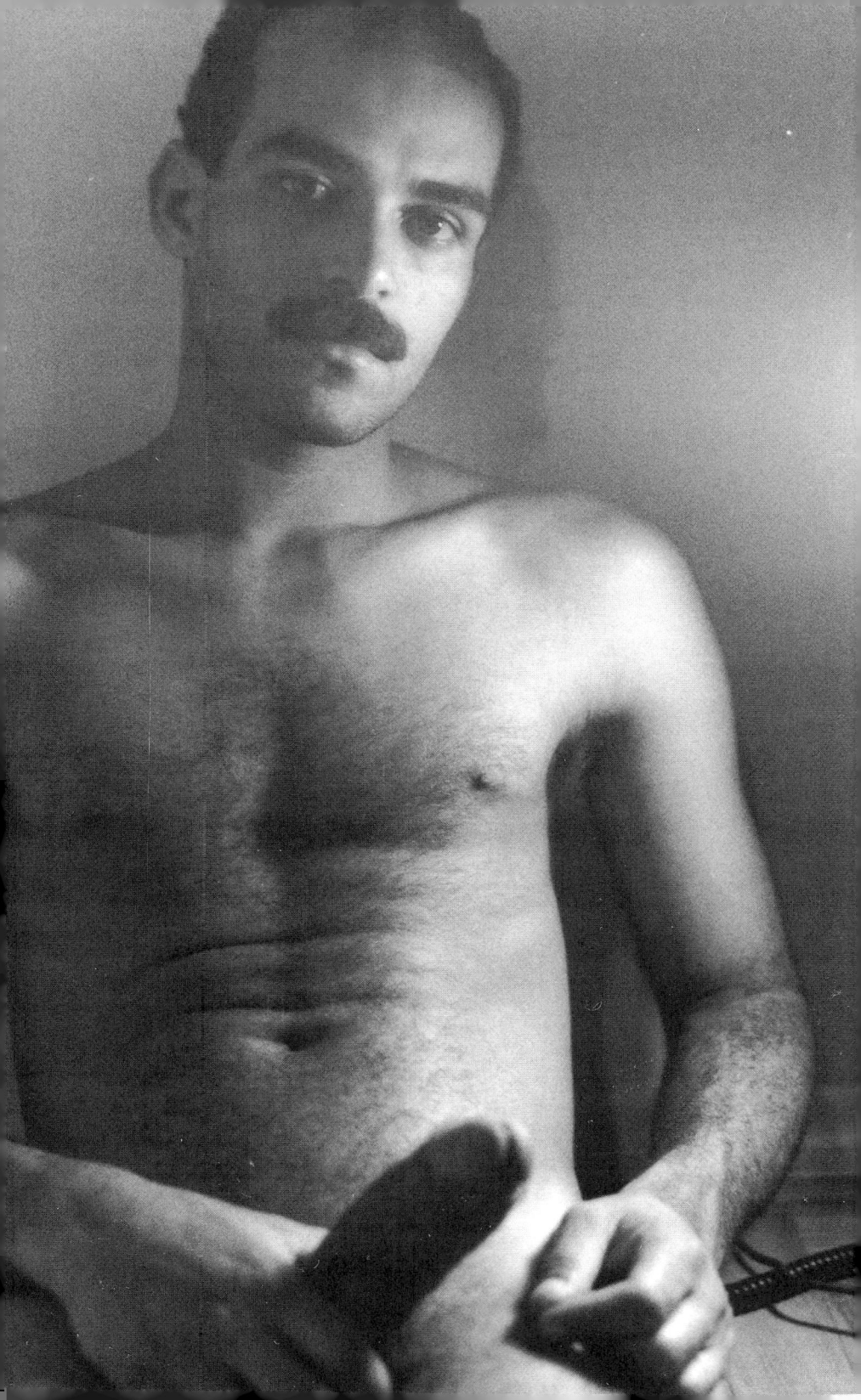

CREAM

True Homosexual Experiences
from S.T.H. Writers
Volume 7

Edited by Boyd McDonald

Leyland Publications
San Francisco

Cover photo copyright © 1995 by Kristen Bjorn
Cover design: Rupert Kinnard
Interior photos: frontispiece & p. 20 copyright © 1995 by Leyland Publications. All other photos (pp. 40, 63, 80, 101, 121, 140, 159, 180) copyright © 1995 by Franco/Ram Studios

All photos shown in this book are posed by professional models. The fact that these models are shown does not imply that they are necessarily homosexual, nor that they endorse any particular code of behavior. The use of the names of well known personages in the text of this book in no way implies that they are to be considered homosexual. The stories presented here are true sexual case histories. The fact that they appear in this book does not mean that the editor or publisher necessarily approve of those acts which may be illegal in some states. It is against the law to have intercourse with boys under 18, but we do print memoirs of men talking about their own boyhood experiences—true case histories in the tradition of Kinsey and the great sex researchers of this country.

ISBN No. 0-943595-55-X

Leyland Publications
P.O. Box 410690
San Francisco, CA 94141
A complete catalogue of available books: $1

THE CASE OF THE
COCK-CRAZY CONSERVATIVE

The Gentleman from Maryland. By Robert Bauman. 276 pages. $17.95. Arbor House.

Capital Hill in Black and White. By Robert Parker with Richard Rashke. 261 pages. $16.95 Dodd, Mead & Company.

Reviewed by Boyd McDonald

Robert Parker, *maitre d'* of the Senate Dining Room, knew four gay senators; ten senators and congressmen were on the particular gay list the cops had in 1980 when Congressman Robert Bauman was charged with violating Section 22-2701 of the District of Columbia Code (solicitation; specifically, solicitation of a young male whore).

In Parker's memoir the Senators have sex right in their offices. In Bauman's the sex takes place all over Washington and Maryland.

Parker is heterosexual and is not disturbed by homosexuality. Bauman is homosexual and is deeply disturbed by it, as is his book.

Congressmen cannot be expected to be openly gay. But Bauman tried to punish other homosexuals, and even a "straight" columnist, Jimmy Breslin, felt it was a bit much that a male who was nabbed on an "oral sodomy" rap should want benefits denied to gay veterans.

It is not as though Bauman did not have good role models. At the early age of six, he had the good fortune to get his cock sucked by Tommy, "a well-built young lad of about 12 or 13" and later there was "Joe," a Pentagon employee who had a house into which he welcomed "a constant stream of neighborhood young toughs, college boys, young male Hill employees, even the Metropolitan police..." Bauman would see Joe with a carful of laughing boys. Sometimes he would join them, but just as often he would try to harm them with legislation.

His education in hypocrisy began at Fork Union Military Academy, Virginia, where "almost" all of the boys had sex with each other and denounced faggots when their mouths were free of cock. Advanced hypocrisy was instilled by Catholicism, to which he still clings today even though he is fully aware of how gay the priesthood is. He cites various estimates that the Catholic clergy is between 30% and 80% gay, and mentions a huge Washington party attended by priests and seminarians. Could as large a group be assembled of priests who like pussy?

In the end he apologizes to his fellow conservatives for betraying them with his homosexuality. It is to other homosexuals that he owes—but does not give in this book—an apology.

There is no question throughout the book which is the stronger force, heterosexuality or homosexuality. He supports heterosexuality while finding it difficult to perform his duty as husband and father, and attacks homosexuality while surrendering repeatedly to its lure. It would take him an hour or two to drive the maid home, even though she lived just ten minutes away; he would use the opportunity to look for meat. He liked naturally muscular young men, not the Schwarzeneggers and Stallones of today.

In fairness to Bauman, who writes less convincingly of traditional American family values than he does of the compulsion to prowl for cock, it should be said that only a shameless bully would attack anything so weak as heterosexuality. Homosexuality can afford his attacks.

Bauman's sexual conquests remain more inspiring than his legislative record. He amassed a sexual record that any healthy homosexual could be proud of—but Bauman is not a healthy homosexual. While sponsoring anti-porn legislation, he stashed gay periodicals under the front seat of his car, where his wife found them, and in the basement, where his four-year-old son found them. As a state legislator in Maryland, he killed a bill that would forbid discrimination against homosexuals, and shacked up with a "handsome blond maintenance man" at the Maryland Inn in Annapolis. In the U.S. Congress he both supported and introduced anti-homosexual measures while regularly indulging his taste for muscular hitchhikers and whores. He had to like both their faces and bodies, he writes, and though he does not mention this, it is clear from his escapades that he liked them tough. When he picked up two hitchhiking Marines and took them to the river, one socked him so hard his teeth cut through, "creating an opening big enough for a finger." Then they "forced" him to drive them back to the marine barracks.

Another hitchhiker "immediately" placed his left hand on Bauman's leg. Bauman drove him to the offices of the American Conservative Union, a magnificently hypocritical place for a blow job. But the hitchhiker turned out to be just as conservative as Bauman; he pulled a knife. There was no money at the American Conservative Union, which was morally bankrupt too, so the hitchhiker said, "All right, queer, take me to your home and we'll see what you have there."

A "handsome, tanned" young man assigned to drive the drunken Bauman home from a party didn't like it when the congressman "made a pass" at him (Bauman fails to specify whether it was a verbal or manual pass) and when he got him home and got the door open he "threw me in."

6

The book gives the strongest support to date to the suspicion that while conservatives are politically uncaring, they do definitely care about cock:

The closets of Washington are full of gay Republicans and gay conservatives. Many of them serve in high Reagan administration posts, some in the White House. They serve in the Congress and populate the circles of power that exist in law firms, public relations firms, lobbying groups, political action committees, even conservative organizations and the Republican party structure . . .

"The top federal consultant on one of the major international issues now current" is gay, and "the son of one of the top U.S. intelligence officials" (whose father has spies following him), and "another board member of Young Americans for Freedom," the organization for educated rednecks. A TV reporter who was "particularly brutal" in exposing Bauman has "a preference" for young male whores. One congressman couldn't hire Bauman as a "consultant" because "the gay thing would really hurt in my state," but Bauman knew that "two of his top aides regularly are seen weekends at Washington gay clubs." A little scene at one such club:

Preppie: "I just got a job on the staff of the subcommittee on such-and-so."
Man: "That's fabulous. I'm a member of that subcommittee."

It is less newsworthy that the Democrats are busily cruising Washington, including the Carter aide who arrived at a "male brothel" on 13th Street N.W. in a chauffeur-driven government limo; Democrats are more caring than Republicans. But Bauman writes, "Frankly I was stunned at the name" of "a very prominent Democratic congressman" who's gay. Bauman "protested" to Congressman Larry McDonald, source of the report, "that he surely must be mistaken." But Lar said it was true for sure.

Nor is it news that many priests are (to use a word Bauman uses absent-mindedly) "bent:"

A priest of my acquaintance regularly leaves his New England parish for weekday evenings in New York's Times Square area where he acquires handsome young males who spend the night with him. More than once he has run into other priests from his area bent upon similar concerns . . .

Congresswoman Gladys Spellman's comment on Bauman was hideously embarrassing (whether from stupidity or viciousness) in light of the activity cops said Bauman proposed, oral sodomy. "I have never," Gladys said, "felt the sting of his tongue, but there are others who have felt that lash."

"Oral sodomy" is a refined phrase for the activity, and most writing about sex is equally refined. Robert Parker, the senate's *maitre d'*, can hardly be expected to go into lascivious detail but he could, when he wrote that "Many an evening I walked into a hideaway (office)... only to find the senator and his male friend sitting in shorts," have specified whether they were boxer or Jockey shorts. To do so would be pleasantly lecherous without being litigious.

When the "gay guest of an important senator from the West" exclaimed, upon seeing Parker, "what a big, handsome black man," Parker "laughed all the way back to the Senate Dining Room." But sex is no laughing matter and "gay" is an imprecise adjective for it. The "gay guest" may well have been the most serious matter taken up that day by the "important senator from the West."

Even more serious was the scene in the office of a "senator from the Deep South" who had three naked male guests. That is *serious*. One of the guests yelled at waitresses who opened the door, "Keep that door shut, you black bitches." While it is admirable to be aggressive even under such embarrassing conditions, it is possible to be aggressive without being abusive, and like Parker, who says that homosexuality on Capitol Hill is "not exactly rare," I'm shocked not at the nudity of the men but at their swinishness.

The incidents with what Lyndon B. Johnson called "pussy" are more detailed yet more tedious; there is a routine quality to heterosexuality and the account of Johnson pinching and slapping the black and white butts of his sluts "so hard that some of the women could hardly walk to the elevator afterward" would be interesting only if the women slapped him back. They should have, poor dears.

The experience of a visiting mayor who wanted "a colored girl" is potentially interesting; he wound up in *The Washington Post* under the headline, ALABAMA MAYOR ROLLED, after waking to find "his wallet, pants, underwear, all of his clothes, even his eyeglasses, stolen." If His Honor was adequately hung and had a nice butt, belly, thighs, and so on, the episode could be interesting, and if not, not.

The brawl between a senator's wife and his fucking secretary, in which "They were both calling each other bitches and worse," raises the question of what Parker means by "worse." That Washington wives could well acquire foul speech from their husbands is suggested by the fact that L.B.J., according to Parker, received reporters while he was taking what he called "a crap." A reporter asked Johnson what he thought of the Berlin crisis. "It stinks," he replied, and added the clarifying remark, "Not my shit, either."

Knowing how dirty the reader is, I have emphasized the sex parts in these books. But equally interesting is Marie German, a Senate Dining Room executive whose "drinking problem was so bad that by early afternoon she could barely walk," Parker writes. "I had to assign a waitress to escort her to the ladies room." The image of Marie drunkenly lunging and lurching about the capitol building is nothing less than enchanting and serves, moreover, as a metaphor for the manner in which the senate conducted all its activities.

Parker's memories of his boyhood in East Texas contribute valuable, but sickening, data to the history of American racism. Parker acquired a patron who was to become powerful, Lyndon B. Johnson. Johnson gave him this advice:

Let me tell you one thing, nigger. As long as you are black, and you're gonna be black till the day you die, no one's gonna call you by your goddam name. So no matter what you are called, nigger, you just let it roll off your back like water, and you'll make it. Just pretend you're a goddam piece of furniture.

Parker's terse summaries of presidents display an historian's gift; certainly his conclusion that John F. Kennedy's "administration was mostly varnish" is more exact than the friendly histories written by the Kennedy court jester, Arthur M. Schlesinger, Jr. Parker sees Reagan, as history doubtless will, as a creature who "has his head in the sand" and who leads an administration that is wallowing in "ignorance."

No one in the other book, except possibly Bauman's friend Joe, is as alluring as Marlon Brando, who, Parker writes, "was a friend of Senator Eugene McCarthy" and who "always stopped in the Senate Dining Room to see me." Brando was especially interesting after he announced that he'd had homosexual experience and before he got fat, but he is not, unhappily, mentioned as being among the men who came to the capitol building to get laid. »«

"I'D LIKE TO, BUT MY WIFE IS PROBABLY BACK."

MISSOURI-The male encounters that I treasure are those few that happen on the spur of the moment, hot and fast, when 2 men meet and recognize the fact that they want to mate, there and now. Of course this doesn't happen often, sometimes once or twice a year, sometimes not for years. This is one that happened. It's true.

I was going to have several buddies over at my house over Labor Day to watch cable TV. Saturday morning early I went to a big supermarket to load up on food and beer for the weekend. I was early, about 15 minutes before the store opened. I sat on a bench near the entrance and tried to write out a list of articles I needed.

A car drove on to the parking lot and out got a big young man over 6 foot, wearing a white undershirt, Levi cutoffs, crew socks and Nikes. He looked like he was BIG all over. There was a woman with him. They came over to the store entrance and moaned when they found they had a quarter of an hour to wait.

They sat down on the bench beside me with him in the middle and when I got a whiff of his body odor, I was a male bitch in heat. Another day and that guy would really stink, but at that moment he had the perfect odor of male sweat. My favorite aphrodisiac.

After some arguing, the woman said she had better take the car and go on some other errand and leave him to buy the groceries, mentioning ham, bread and beer. She kept giving him instructions such as to be sure to have the ham sliced, the brand of beer somebody preferred, and so on. They stood up, he gave her the car keys, she cautioned him again to get the right groceries, gave him a kiss, and wrinkling up her nose told him he stunk. A 3-day weekend camping, she said, and you already smell like a goat. Then she left, and the hunk and I were left sharing a bench in front of Kroger's.

He turned to me and sort of grinned and said the old saw about can't live with 'em and can't live without 'em. I said I was doing very well without 'em and he said "Oh."

He touched his hand to his groin lightly. I took the plunge and stared openly at his crotch, even licked my lips a little. He noticed and the hand went to the groin again, briefly. I felt like jumping right on him (and maybe get the shit beat out of me, too). Then the damn store opened. Oh, yes, I forgot—we had also talked about the beautiful new red van with orange flames painted on it that was sitting on the parking lot and which I told him was my van. He said he wanted to take a look at it, if he had time after buying the groceries. And we had talked about the baseball situation also. (Straight men like cars and

10

sports better than sex, I've found.) Incidentally, the van was my brother's, and that was the only day I drove it. My brother and his wife had to drive in a funeral procession that afternoon and my sister-in-law had decided that my black Ford Fairmont would look better at a funeral than a bright red and orange van.

We went into the store and I met him again in the meat section. I helped him pick out a ham and even gave it to the butcher to be sliced. I stuck close to him through about 20 minutes of shopping, feeling feverish, ogling his groin, rubbing against him in the aisles. I was sure he was hip. I was sure he knew what I wanted. Once, when we were the only 2 people in an aisle, I cupped my hand and held it about 6 inches from his crotch. He moved forward until my hand was on his groin. I groped him, he was on his way to getting a hard on, and I said, "Let's go out to my van."

"No way," he said. "I don't have time."

I felt him up a little more between our shopping carts. He said, "Hell, I'd like to, but my wife is probably back already."

So that was all. I had tried. We parted. He even went to a different checkout counter. I checked out, paid my bill, put my groceries in the van, but waited. And waited. And waited.

Then the hunk came out of the store and approached me. Yes, he was coming my way!

"Hey fellow," he said, "Can you do me a favor? You're the only person I know around here and I need somebody to drive me to where my car is stalled. My wife just phoned the store. Will you drive me there?"

I had long ago thrown all caution to the winds; I said, "Yes—as soon as I've sucked your cock."

He got in the back of the van, I parked in a safe place, unzipped those bulging cutoffs and slipped them down over his massive thighs. The cock was a hard 5 inches but thick, very thick. Almost too thick. And that smell. Oh, that smell. And the taste—pissy, spermy, sweaty cock. And the load, spurting and plentiful, strong and raunchy and potent tasting.

I'm hard right now thinking of that smell and taste. Maybe I won't run into this kind of action for a long time. But it's the best thing that happened to me this year.

"HOLY COW! YOU HAVE A LOT OF COME."

CALIFORNIA – My college fraternity hs a honey of a policy toward its alumni. Any alumnus can, no matter how old, come back and use the fraternity house. We are lifetime members. Naturally the alumni leave handsome contributions.

I'm most drawn to teenagers, physically that is. That was true when I was in college and is still true now. But I learned during the first homecoming that the older guys could be really sexy. It wasn't the big fall homecoming—it was in June at commencement time, about a month after I'd been initiated. I'd just turned 19.

Some of the older alumni were so obviously excited about visiting the fraternity house that I became interested too. There wasn't much about its earlier stages to suggest that it was any more than a lot of men reminiscing about their college days. I guess there must have been about 20 alumni there from various years.

Up until midnight it was a completely open party. Anybody could have walked in and would have observed nothing more than comradery, as in other fraternity houses. At midnight, however, the lights were turned low. Guys either wandered off or stayed, whatever they wanted.

I'd gotten to talking late in the evening with a keen-eyed man of about 50. I'll call him Harold. He had dark hair and a dark moustache. My first thought was that he was old enough to be my father but quickly I felt like a contemporary with him, talking about what I was doing, what I was interested in, and the career I hoped to follow. From that we drifted, when the lights were dimmed, to talking about our sex experiences. Sitting in the dim light with him, I began to feel the magnetism of his body.

Finally, Harold said, "Well, I think I'm going to turn in. You're welcome to come with me."

I'd been moving toward this idea for some time. "Yeah," I said. "I'd like that."

As soon as I said it, I felt scared. I guess I thought of "adults" as something quite different from myself—authority figures, not lovers. What an eye-opener I would have found in "Memoirs of a Headmaster" in your book. I would have realized that boys and men are moved by identical feelings. Harold did that for me.

He also taught me that sex could be light-hearted and casual, something I'd forgotten since early childhood. He was extremely relaxed. When we got to his hotel he didn't whip off his clothes in that urgent way that many anxious teenagers do. I remember he did slip off his shoes, then got a bottle of sherry out of his suitcase and poured two drinks.

Then he returned to the sex conversation we'd been having at the fraternity house. With that, my heart stopped pounding and I began to let the action set its own pace. When he finally began to undress, I felt as if I were with a roommate. He was spare, well-muscled. He went into the bathroom and I heard the shower. I stripped, now with a casualness I wouldn't have expected. When he came out still drying himself I felt pleasure in walking past him naked into the bathroom.

The low-wattage bed lamp was on when I came out and slipped into bed beside him. "My, you look smooth," he said, his eyes on my hairless chest. As I lay on my back our arms and legs touched and the warmth of his skin made my cock hard, pointing not at the ceiling but at some spot above my head. Ordinarily in the presence of an adult I'd have been embarrassed but he was taking it as something natural. He bent over me and touched his tongue to my nipples, which promptly came out of their flattened condition and hardened. Now I began to feel really on fire and was ready for anything.

But he took his time, though I could feel his hard cock against my hip. He kissed me lightly. He talked to me during the early stages; he asked a question and I was thinking about the answer and then suddenly his hand was between my legs and playing with my balls. He played me like a musical instrument. He finally started sucking my cock. Several times, just as I thought I was passing the point of no return, he would withdraw and I'd feel his hairy head against my stomach. Each time he'd start again, licking my cock and balls, and then I'd feel that exciting mouth slip over the head of my cock and slide down it. Finally he made a final pass up and down my cock, his mouth as tight as an asshole, and I came.

When we pulled apart he said, "Holy cow! You have a lot of cum."

I met Harold again at the fall reunion, just after the war, and much later when I returned for a reunion in the late 70s. I was 56 then and he had to be about 87. The boys were attentive to us both. We decided to sleep together again. He was thin, his skin was slack, but in bed he was still an exciting man.

When he died two years ago, he left his sizeable estate to the fraternity.

I can imagine that the other fraternities have wondered what magic made our alumni so loyal. I hope they never find out.

"HE WANTED HIS ASS LICKED."

SAN ANTONIO–I am 66 years old. I am six feet and weigh between 175 and 180. I have 6 1/2 inches. I am in good health. I have been retired for six years. I was in the U.S. Army for 21 years. Then I lived in the Republic of South Africa for 16 years. I worked for the South Africa Department of Health. I have been living in lovely San Antonio, Texas for almost six years.

My wife of 40 years was born in London, England. We met in 1944 in a London blackout. We had two sons. Our youngest was killed in an automobile accident about 10 years ago. We have another son who lives in Houston, Texas.

My wife and I, by mutual consent, no longer have any sex. She was never too happy with having sex and after the children were born, for some reason I became impotent. *I am not so now, let me assure you!* My wife knows and my son most likely knows that I am gay. But, as I am kind, generous, patient and loving with both of them, they do not condemn me for something that I cannot help and I would not like to be anything else but gay.

I go to the steam baths each Saturday. There is a group of eight of us, all "bound" together with the understanding that we will only have sex within our own group of eight. This way we feel that our chances of getting AIDS or any other disease are lessened. There is a chance, of course, that one or more of our group will "fall" and go with someone else. But I MUST go each week. Sometimes I go also on midweek days. I usually have six sexual partners each Saturday. Less during my midweek visits. With the six partners, I usually come two or three times.

I love fucking—the "top man" role. All of my group of sex partners like to be the bottom man, so I am all right. I of course like to be sucked and rimmed and I like sixty-nine. I like to caress, feel, hug, kiss, cuddle and show another man that I care for him. I am honest, kind, generous, very clean (I have just finished taking the second hepatitis B injections). I will never cheat, steal or be haughty with my friends. I do not smoke or take drugs. I drink about five drinks in a week.

As a retired military man I had little experience in the gay world and hoped to find what I had missed for the past 20 years. Being very discreet and cautious, I decided to take in a Bath in S.A., not knowing much about the layout that first time. However, I was horny and dared to try.

It was on a weekday in the afternoon and no one could be seen wandering around in the halls. After my shower I went back to my locker and as I was leaving a middle aged man came in. He saw me and said, "What a nice looking ass you have."

I looked over and he looked like he had too many drinks and could hardly stand up. He then said, "I would like to fuck that ass of yours." He wasn't bad looking and I said, "I bet you couldn't get that cock of yours hard enough to fuck anything." He said, "That's a bet."

I left and went to the T.V. room and watched a porn movie. I cruised around in hope of finding someone to my liking. After he had his shower, the drunk came looking for me. I was standing in a large semi dark room with mattresses on the floor when he grabbed me from behind with both arms around me. "You lose your bet," he said. "My cock is hard and I am going to fuck you."

I said, "I have never been fucked before and I was only joking." He pushed me down on the mattress and said, "I don't joke and you are going to get fucked."

I said, "Please, sir, I'll jack you off. Will that do?" "No way," he said. Since he had a nice, hard big cock I said, "If you wish I'll even suck it for you."

He shoved my head down on his cock and said for me to start sucking. I went down on my knees and took the huge head of his cock into my mouth and sucked on it, but that wasn't good enough for him. He wanted his ass licked and sucked. A couple of wacks on my ass and I obeyed orders. After I had served his desires he turned me over and slowly penetrated my asshole with his huge cock. It hurt at first but then as time went on it felt satisfying. He fucked me for what seemed like a half hour until he was ready to come and then pulled his cock out and shoved it into my mouth. I gagged and choked but he made me suck it.

All the time my cock was hard and ready. I was so horny and wanted to get my rocks off. But he never once gave me any play. If he had I would have shot my wad.

He shot his load in my mouth and told me to keep it in my mouth and taste it awhile and then swallow it. I obeyed.

He went to shower and I have never seen him since.

AT WEEKEND CAMP.

CALIFORNIA – The first time I ever took a cock in my ass, neither I nor my partner, another Boy Scout, knew anything whatever about lubricants or about giving the sphincter time to relax. We both wanted it to the point of being out of our heads.

I'd been fantasizing about it ever since I first heard of the idea over two years earlier. Erle, with whom I'd been 69-ing for the last three weekend camps, was primed for action from the moment the guys gathered in the Scoutmaster's house on Saturday morning and I whispered what I wanted.

The troop had a lodge on a lake northeast of town. The structure had a broad inside balcony around three sides, and all our cots, including the Scoutmaster's, were crowded in here.

Erle and I picked the afternoon swim time for our experiment, virtuously explaining that I wanted to help him learn fire-by-friction for a test he had to pass. We had the sets with us to make the story more convincing.

And so, while everyone else was down at the lake, we went up to the balcony and stripped. Erle was a year younger than I and smaller. I guess he was average hung. He was circumcized and of course already hard. I got down on my knees on the floor and bent over the side of my cot. It was exciting to feel his tip probing around my asshole and then pressing against the hole.

Erle got anxious. "I can't get in," he said.

"Push," I said.

He pressed and suddenly I yelled like a stuck pig. He thought he'd seriously injured me and quickly pulled out, making me roar even louder. Only the head of his cock had been inside me, but that was enough.

Both our cocks softened rapidly. But when it was clear that my injury wasn't permanent, we sat on the floor and laughed till we were almost hysterical.

Little by little we warmed to one another again—after all, we were alone and naked. We went downstairs, washed our cocks at the pump, came back up, and sucked one another off.

Oh, yes, we revved up the fire-by-friction sets, so there would be a smell of burnt wood and shavings in the air when the swimmers got back.

"He has me lick his balls and asshole."

When I lie down in bed at night I frequently have a fantasy that my hands and feet are tied and that in this helpless state I am about to be fucked or sucked or made to suck a man more powerful than I. It's a most voluptuous feeling. Looking back at my life, I can see how often I experienced this either by chance or by my own maneuvering.

My first recollection is of a time too early for me to remember how old I was. In a game of cowboys and Indians I was tied up and I still recall the immediate pleasure.

Even where I have not been bound or "over-powered," I can see that I've played a passive role or have tried to draw someone else into "seducing" me or "taking" me with at least a hint of physical force.

Oscar, my Scout patrol leader when I was in my early teens, suited my needs perfectly, for he seemed to have the opposite compulsion— to overpower, to dominate, to father. How many times he made me wrestle with him! Apart from the fact that he sometimes hurt me, I delighted in these encounters, which always ended up with me on my back being pressed into submission by his body, smelling of sweat. In these situations I'd get hard ons that somehow never seemed embarrassing, even though I was at an age when I would get sudden hard ons in public places for no apparent reason and would be acutely embarrassed by them and would go to great lengths to conceal them.

When I got my own pup tent, I set it up in the backyard and from time to time slept out there with friends. Once I was in it with a younger, very high-strung boy with the odd name of Jewel. We were going to sleep in some kind of clothing, either our underwear or pajamas, and I proposed a game in which I would try to "pants" him and if I didn't succeed he could sock me in the jaw. I no sooner touched him than he flew into a fury of struggling and, as I anticipated, I was quickly the one who was naked. I told him to go ahead and hit me, but he was basically a gentle person and he just gave me a light tap. I pretended to be knocked out and lay there beside him on my back, my cock standing up like a flagpole. The innocent child promptly fell asleep!

My fraternity initiation couldn't have suited my inclinations better, with its wrestling and binding. My later experiences in the fraternity, while wonderful, seldom matched the excitement of the initiation, for the reason that sex was accepted so matter-of-factly later on. There were so many blow jobs in the fraternity that it was too normal and wholesome to have that special effect on me I get when I'm *made* to have sex.

I have had the same lover now for 22 years, a former student. We can get together only infrequently because of marriage, occupation, and geography; but when we do our love-making falls into that pattern of forced sex so congenial to me. It's about three-quarters congenial to Terry too because he's naturally aggressive. But he's also very kind, and though he's a professional actor, he's not completely convincing as a master bending me to his will. He has a lean, powerful physique that makes me start to submit even as I look at it. Typically, he might order me to kneel in front of him. With a show of roughness he pulls my face into his crotch, and has me lick his balls and asshole. Then I'm on my back and he is squatting over my face. He is always squeaky clean, with not a hint of smell unless it's a faint fragrance of Right Guard.

Then he's on his back hugging me with his legs as I lick his cock. When I have sucked him off, he will suck me off.

"I think he was straight."

As a student, hitchhiking home from Stanford, after many rides I finally got one with a fellow about my own age, driving a model A Ford. I think this was in Oklahoma. His name was Perry, short for Peregrine, and I think he was straight.

He wanted to drive night and day and even taught me to drive so that he could nap between stretches at the wheel. He was broad-shouldered and muscular but not chunky. His hair I remember was tan rather than brown or blond. I wouldn't say he was handsome but he was pleasing to look at.

We got along beautifully. None of that irritation that builds up between two guys after a long time in each other's company.

We never talked about sex or made any move toward one another, and nothing might have happened if we hadn't gotten into a terrific rainstorm and the water splashed up and caused the engine to conk out. This happened repeatedly and Perry would let the car sit for awhile and then re-start it. Finally he decided we'd better wait out the storm and so we stopped at a farm house that advertised rooms.

Perry asked for twin beds but only a double was available, so we took it. We took a very soothing bath in a tub—separately—and got into bed. Perry went right off to sleep and I wasn't long after him.

So far I'd been very restrained, despite my prior promiscuous behavior. He seemed—indeed he was—not interested. But after an hour or two I woke up and became terribly conscious of him lying beside me. He hadn't made a single suggestive remark or move, but as I lay there my cock got hard as a rock and I became more and more excited. Even so, I was inhibited enough that I wouldn't have done anything if he hadn't, in turning over, flung his arm over my waist. Oh, did that feel good!

I lay there, my heart pounding, waiting for his hand to move on me. But it didn't and after a short time he rolled over and away from me.

I was just crazy with excitement and decided I had to touch him. I

18

edged closer. The whole transit across a foot of bed must have taken me 10 minutes. Finally my chest touched his back and my head was on his pillow just behind his own head. Not a sign of his being awakened. I inched my belly closer till I felt the tip of my cock touching the crack of his ass just where the cheeks slope down into the thighs. Still he was deep in sleep. I pressed forward and now my shaft (which is five or six inches, depending on whether you measure it from above or beneath) was in contact along its length with the crack between his cheeks.

It was scary. I slipped my left arm over his waist, rationalizing that I was doing no more than he'd done earlier.

I lay like that for a long time. When it appeared that he was still asleep, I moved my hand up to touch his chest, which I'd admired so much when he was undressing. His nipples were 3 or 4 times the size of mine, and as I gently touched them, they hardened.

I tried to move my hand so slowly that it would not seem to be moving, but would just be in a new position if noticed. It was a long, slow, terribly exciting trip from his chest down to his belly button to his pubic hair and finally to the base of his cock. By now I simply could not stop myself.

I slid his underpants off.

I'm not a size queen but in this case I was awed. First, it was very thick. I couldn't touch the tip of my thumb and forefinger in encircling it near the base.

I don't know what its length was but I'm sure it was a good two inches longer than mine. It was still soft, but heavy. Sometimes a cock is so soft you almost feel you could flatten it. This one was full and firm like a thick steak.

Still kidding myself that I could explain my way out of it if necessary, I let my palm rest loosely against his shaft, as though it were there by chance. The surface was like velvet. Gradually I felt his cock hardening, and for the first time I heard Perry moan. I'm convinced he was still asleep at this point. Now I wasn't kidding even myself. I started sliding my palm up and down the shaft from the hair to the big round head. It was now sticking straight out from his belly and I could hear Perry, who had slept silently before, breathing heavily.

His hips began to move in rhythm with my hand on his cock. I became panic-stricken; he would certainly awaken and discover what I was trying to do. But Perry saved the day—or rather night. His hips never stopped moving. In fact they moved faster so that his cock was sliding rapidly in the grip of my left hand. Then I felt his big hand against mine, forcing it to tighten around the shaft of his cock. Now he was supplying all the power, pumping his cock through my hand. In less than a minute he stopped and I felt his sperm rushing up through his shaft.

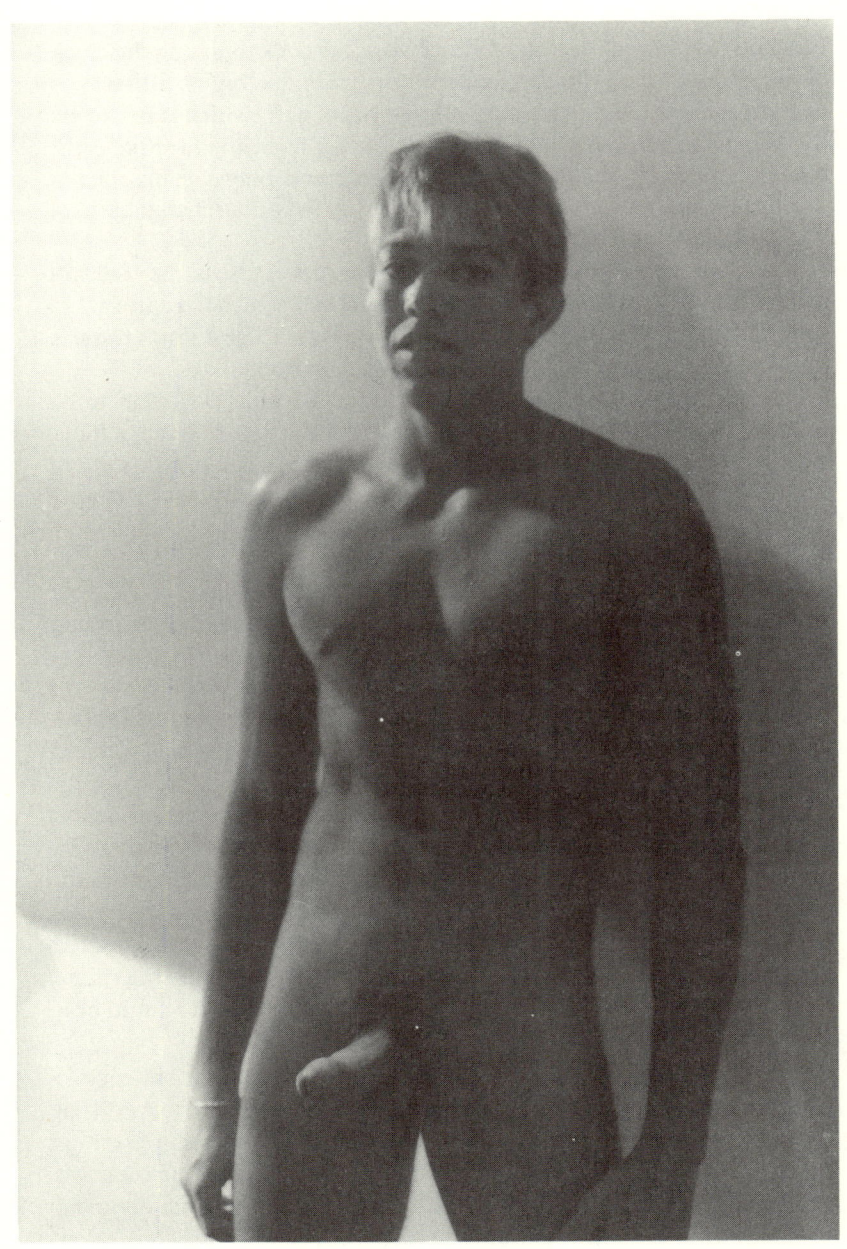

"THOSE BIG GUYS WALKING ABOUT IN JOCK STRAPS."

MANHATTAN – At first, I always picked out meek and gentle looking guys because I felt they would be easy on me. However, in reality, it was the rough and tough type that really fascinated me. One day I thought I would experiment with a guy of this type. I was about 28 then and had been experimenting in this new type of pleasure for about a year.

The guy was a handsome, big, strong guy, and it didn't take long for him to persuade me to go to his apartment with him (this was back in the late 50s before things were so bad). However, when he tried to fuck me with that monster of a tool he had, I just couldn't take it. He was built like a horse. We tried everything—lubrications, spit, Vaseline, olive oil, soap, but nothing worked. It was just too big for me; the pain was unbearable. I was really quite frightened because this guy was becoming more and more impatient with me.

He finally said, "You ain't gonna get away with this so easy. You got me all hot and bothered and you're gonna go through with something. If you can't take it from the rear, you're gonna have to take it from the front."

I had never actually committed fellatio before—maybe in my dreams, but not with a man. I always remembered Communion Sundays, when preparing to take Communion, and the Pastor would say, "He who drinks from this cup unworthily, drinks damnation to his soul." I could in no way reconcile putting both these objects into my mouth: the holy Communion Cup and a guy's cock.

However, my friend was becoming more and more hostile. As he was a bit drunk, I didn't know what he might do to me if I didn't please him. "O.K.," I finally said, "I'll let you put it into my mouth, but take it out when you feel yourself starting to come, O.K.?" He agreed.

So I got on my back and he stretched out his big frame over me and began to pump with all his force. I thought I would choke to death. I couldn't move or get out of the way as he was over twice my size. Finally, I knew he was beginning to come and I squirmed and tried to indicate with gurgles and gags that he had promised to take it out. But he didn't pay any attention. He was breathing like a bull and the sweat was draining down from his body. His heavy underarm odor mingled with the tobacco and gin smell of his breath and the sweaty, heady, musty odor of his crotch. Then he exploded and a liquid, salty and slightly bitter, slid down my throat. I tried to keep from swallowing it but since he was still on top of me and I couldn't move or turn my head, it was either swallow or strangle. He held me there firmly and completed emptying all his load into my mouth. It seemed like a long time before he got up.

I hurried home; washed my mouth out real good with Listerine, and "prayed penance" for several days. However, I never forgot that moment. From that day on, when I was broken in, I have been a confirmed lover of getting fucked in the mouth.

I was reared in a very small town in northern Ohio and was brought up in a very religious family. In our family even reading the funny papers on Sunday was considered a sin, so you can imagine how negative any views of homosexuality were. Throughout my childhood, people of the "third sex" were considered "funny" people and we children were sternly warned to beware of them.

However, I noticed from an early age that I enjoyed looking at the ads for underwear in the old Spiegel, May, Stern, and Montgomery Ward catalogues. In those days not much of a bulge was made for the crotch but I imagined it was there, anyway.

I also used to gape at the big football heroes as they would lumber out on the football field. My eyes were always on their biceps and their crotches. At the time I did not know why, but now, looking back over it, I realize what I wanted.

I used to go into the locker room of the gym where the guys were practicing (my big brother played football on the high school team and would take me to watch the practice sessions). I just savored the odor of the sweat. The smell of the gym exhilarated me and seeing those big guys walking about in towels and jock straps excited me no end.

"I'M MARRIED TOO."

DELAWARE–I have a few curious experiences from visits to the "adult" book store movie booths that might amuse your readers. There are two book stores in the area with glory holes. One has square-shaped holes big enough to get your arm through and big enough to accommodate a good pair of balls along with the cock. The other store has round holes only big enough to get the cock through. Both stores have booths larger in size than those with the glory holes so if two guys really want to get it on, they can go in the big booths (and save money, too).

Some guys are really up tight about being seen going in a booth with another guy so in that case, timing is very important. There are always a few drooling men around who are hard to shake and patience and will power are necessary.

One day I watched a young guy, somewhat on the stocky side but interesting, as he went from one booth to another—those with no glory holes. I was about to give up on him when I saw him enter one of the booths with a glory hole. I went into the other one and put in my quarter, then knelt to peer through the hole at him. He was leaning against the opposite wall and looked at me with a rather startled expression.

I beckoned to him with my fingers, smiling and licking my lips, but he didn't respond although I could see a growing bulge in his pants. So—shamelessly—I reached through to touch him but he backed away. I whispered, "Let me suck it." He said, "I'll let you feel it, that's all," and moved closer.

I felt his pants, rubbing the big hard on through the fabric, then pulled down the zipper, reached in and fumbled with his Jockey shorts and finally pulled out a very nice cut cock about 6 inches long.

As I massaged it, it grew and got harder. I pulled it to the opening where I licked the head of it. He responded by pushing it through the opening. I could hear him breathing hard and I was reassured by his continuing to feed quarters to his movie that he was going to stay with me.

It didn't take too many thrusts down on his cock till he exploded into my mouth. He left it there for a few minutes before pulling away and making a fast exit.

Another time I followed a rather tall guy around, and when nobody else was in sight I invited him to share a big booth with me. He accepted readily and brought out a big cut dick for me to suck. I took it in my mouth, then undid his belt and pulled his pants and Jockeys down to his ankles. Then I kissed his legs and balls and sucked cock and balls till he grabbed his cock, jerked it about four times and poked it into my mouth, where he shot a big load.

All of this is not unusual, but as he was pulling himself back together he said, "Are you clean?" I said, "What?" He said, "I mean, I hope you're clean; I'm married."

I thought, now's a funny time for him to be asking this, but I said to him, "Well, I hope you are clean, too. I'm married too." He said, "Well, you have to be careful when you're married." What struck me as funny was that he hadn't thought to ask *before* he had his fun—afterwards, it would have been too late anyhow. I've seen him there a couple of times since and we repeat the scene, but now he just says, "I know you're clean!"

TAKES JOB BATHING, DRESSING 22-YEAR-OLD.

I'd like to relate an experience I had about 10 yrs. ago when I was 22. It's a bit off the wall for publication, but very special to me as it fulfilled one of my deepest fantasies. Certainly a dream come true.

While drifting around Miami, I answered an ad in the newspaper for a part time job as a "counselor" for a private party. Not knowing quite what to expect, I was given an address & arrived on time at a seedy run down 4 unit apt. bldg. I rang the doorbell and a Boris Karloff looking man in his 40s answered & invited me in.

It was a hot summer afternoon; inside all the shades were closed. There was no air conditioning & the familiar odor of vomit was quite prevalent. Also the place was a mess with junk all over & stacks of books & mags everywhere.

As I sat down on the couch I noticed in the dim light what appeared to be about a 16 yr. old boy playing on the floor with a train set. He was short, husky (a little out of shape), but an unusually handsome face, sort of like James Dean, but much better looking.

I could tell immediately there was something very wrong with him as he moodily stared at me & then started to cry. Needless to say it was love at first sight for me.

Anyway, the man explained to me that he was a schizophrenic who had not spoken since he was five (was actually 22—same as me) & had spent most of his life in maximum security as he had a violent temper if provoked. He needed to be watched 24 hours a day & I was to stay with him from 12 noon to 11 at nite while the man went to work (at a mental hospital). I gathered that he had gotten him out of the hospital to try & rehabilitate him.

I was not immediately hired which devastated me as I would have done the job for nothing, but received a call about 3 days later to report for work.

My first day at work was a harrowing experience as he hallucinated a great deal, suffering one minute and then appearing to be very happy and always nothing to do but sit around the apartment or walk around the block. Because of his obvious condition,people stared at us while we were out.

I was supposed to teach him to write or read, but it was rather hopeless. That evening after feeding him—he ate just hamburgers and very cold cokes and chain smoked Salems—I was sitting on the couch next to him with my leg against his wondering if there was any hope, when he abruptly got up and went into the bedroom.

After a couple of minutes I got up to look and there he was lying stomach down on the bed lustily grinding his hips in what appeared to be obvious sexual movements (his clothes were on).

Getting very excited myself, I walked over to the bed and he strongly motioned me out of the room. So I left the room rather disheartened.

I had never had a real sexual experience myself (a real closet case) and wouldn't have known what to do anyway, so I gave up on that idea and was content just to be around him.

Then, about my 3rd or 4th day at work, I had taken him to the beach (so hot) and we returned about 2:30. I went into the bedroom and layed on the bed on my back. For some reason, I got a hard on which I didn't try to hide (usually I'm very shy). It could be seen through my swimming trunks (shirt was off, too) and that did the trick. He walked in and immediately noticed it and without much hesitation got on the bed and almost immediately layed right on top of me, putting his hands in mine and starting to move his hips like I saw that first day. Then he stuck his tongue down my mouth and I was definitely in heaven and came quickly in my pants.

I think I had about 3 or 4 more encounters with him (with our pants down next time) and also got to bathe him thoroughly and dry him off and dress him. He wouldn't do anything himself just because he didn't want to. He could voluntarily vomit his hamburgers and opened 1/2 gallon milk containers had to be strategically placed around the apartment to catch it.

After about 2 months, he had to be sent back to the mental hospital for disturbing the peace. I was heartbroken at this doomed affair, but have many happy memories of a tender sweet boy who society thought of as a caged crazy animal.

I never thought I'd have another experience like this one, but about five years later, I met another person with similar problems, and that lasted for about 4 years—something I never thought I would survive.

"IT WAS ALL X—RATED"

MANHATTAN–I knew Charles and Gary slightly because they would come into a bar heavily peopled by those of my persuasion although not allout queer. One of the customers invited me to a "get together" at which Charles and Gary were present. It was a dull hen party and I was ready to split at the same time Charles and Gary were ready to split and they asked me if I would care to stop by their place for a nightcap.

It was taken for granted at the bar that Charles and Gary were lovers and I knew that the invitation meant a dash of spice in their ongoing friendship.

They were in their mid-twenties and attractive, slightly overage preppies. I was busily engaged in administering to the needs of various and sundry neighborhood boys and I said yes a drink would go well.

"Lover" in queer circles is an umbrella term. I discovered after accepting the invitation that (1) Gary was indeed Charles's lover, had been for seven years, and (2) Charles was an excellent cocksucker. The spice in the encounter consisted of Gary taking care of business as usual while Charles sucked me off, a most welcome change in my current pattern. We parted after this agreeable go-round, promising vaguely to get together again.

I ran into Charles a few weeks later at the bar. It was during one of Gary's road trips, business taking him out of town about once a month. When Charles asked me home for a drink I said yes, hoping for a blow job, and ended up taking over from Gary, fucking Charles for all I was worth. I stayed overnight, got some head in the morning, and without planning became Charles's other lover.

I should say that in a lifetime of partnering with other males, I have had two of whom I could say that they were my lovers. About them— more later. To be a lover one must perform as a male, more or less regularly, and above all completely. In this sense for a week out of every month I was Charles's lover.

Lest the euphoria of being butch carry me away, there was Manuel to bring me down on my knees in the laundry room of the building wherein Charles and Gary lived. Manny was 20, Hispanic, and an infrequent encounter in the nearby park. He was on the maintenance staff of the building and we quickly renewed our acquaintance on the nights he worked and I visited Charles.

Manny told me that Charles had made moves toward him but he thought it better not to "mess around with the tenants." Just as well, because although I hate to admit it, Charles was an even better cocksucker than I.

A few months later I ran into Gary at the bar. It was the first time I'd seen him since our threesome. I was diffident when we greeted one another but if he knew I was screwing his boyfriend he gave no indication. He said he was a bachelor for a few days because Charles was down south visiting his parents. He asked me if I'd like to come home for a drink.

Gary, as I've said, was an attractive man and I figured I owed him some pussy for all I'd been getting but I hesitated making reference to the fact that he wore the pants in the family. Ruefully, he acknowledged the fact, saying that he wore the pants while Charles was "the head of the household." And then, edging closer to me, he said, "Outside the family I sometimes enjoy taking off my pants."

I went home with him and screwed the shit out of him. The head he gave me later wasn't on par with Charles's but earnest and well-meant. I became his outside-the-family lover.

Fucking these guys, keeping up with my neighborhood boys, and taking care of Manuel was pretty taxing. I enjoyed every minute. When Charles returned and Gary took off it was Charles with Manny sometimes for dessert. When Gary was in town he took to lying to Charles to have the time to come to my place. Sometimes he would tell Charles he was taking off tonight instead of tomorrow and then spending the night under me in my bed. The next night and for the next week I was plunging my dick into Charles.

At first, getting into Gary was particularly exhilarating. How often do you get to fuck a basically macho man? But as time went on the hankering for his dick that began way back during our threesome kept growing. Gary seemed content to be my bitch and I was reluctant to change the status quo. One night after six months of it I decided to act. Charles was away visiting relatives again. He had been gone about two weeks and I figured Gary might be ripe for nookie. I surprised him by going down on him—the very first time. He warmed to this approach and was instantly sympathetic. "I guess you feel like taking the pants off," he joked, and in no time his dick was deep in my shit-hole. I was getting very little up there at the time and Gary was a champ. I stayed overnight and later sucked him off while he ate my pussy.

Gary was pleased with the shift in our partnership and from then on lovers was the correct word for us. Charles had another week away and Gary made up for lost time, jazzing me regularly and well.

When Charles came back I began shit-holing Gary again, but no hard and fast rule—whoever wanted what, got it.

I asked Gary why he didn't have a similar arrangement. He said, "Charles is strictly a cream puff who would be ticked off it he knew I wasn't always butch." He started to talk about splitting with Charles but I was able to persuade him not to. Neither Gary nor I was cut out to be a full-time bitch and if we made it steady the fun would fade. Gary for me was wild all-out sex and we were alike that way. Charles and Gary were friends as well as partners. Withus it was all X-rated. So we kept on digging each other's frame, fucking Charles, and I kept on sucking Manny and every neighborhood lad I could get.

I asked Manny home a few times but he was strictly an on-the-job kid and laundry-room head was good enough for him. So Gary remained in sole custody of my cunt. He and Charles the only heirs to my dick. These were salad days, remember, and Manny and the neighborhood boys supplied the dressing. There is nothing like a balanced diet.

YOUTH SUCKED IN "STRAIGHT" STEAM ROOM

OK here's two true story submissions. Sorry for the scribbling but you get these facts for nothing (anyway).

I had just been "into" some gay play for a short while when I discovered a beachside bath in Brooklyn and this is what happened one day.

I was sunning, nude like everyone else, on the rooftop sundeck. I had gotten there a short while ago and I was on the blanket of a gay friend. Me, I am bi. My friend was (is) a real cockworshipper and I am not the slightest bit surprised if I turn around and find him down on me. Sure, I enjoy it and he's a fine cocksucker.

Well, today a different fellow, stranger, comes over to speak to us. We're all nude and I am lying on my back with my head propped up. I notice that as the new fella speaks to us his eyes seem to spend the most time looking at my body. Although a senior man himself I liked his body and his prick looked nice.

One thing to be mentioned here is that this place is *not a gay bath,* although there is regular discreet gay action in the dressing rooms.

The stranger's name is John and he offers to put lotion on my back. I accept wondering if he's there "for action." He applies it over to my ass but does so in a non-sensual way.

Well, we lose contact for a while and the next time I see him is just after I had left the shower, washing up after David, my friend, had just blown me.

28

John follows me to my dressing room. I leave the door open and he begins speaking to me. He says he likes me and reaches over and takes hold of my soft dick. He fondles it and my balls with both his hands. I remark "I'm sorry but I just came." He says maybe we meet later? I tell him "I don't know."

Later on, while showering off from the sun, he says hello and asks to wash my back. He washes my back; and then my ass, and into my crack. He slips his soapy finger into my hole and washes it. A second finger joins the first. He's got me breathing hard now and we are discovered, thankfully by another gay gent. The fellow smiles at John and says musically "Fun in the shower" and cautions us to *be careful*.

John continues with his fingers in my ass until we're almost discovered by a straight fellow. We walk smartly into the steam room and find it crowded. Straights, gays, bis, voyeurs, you name it. John guides me to the back and he sits on the bench. John stood me in front of him. I was self conscious when John put his fingers back into my behind. I just prayed that all the fellas seeing this were gay. A small line of 3 understanding men stood in front of me effectively hiding me from the steam room population. At that, John turned, placing my left hip side against his right chest. Angling my hard on toward him he quickly went down on it. The blowing was a delight and during it the fingers went back into my anus; rubbing, spreading, and stimulating it.

I was loving the entire experience and then all of a sudden the single light bulb in the ceiling went out. After the initial surprise, we all realized it was completely dark. Fearlessly John resumed blowing me. John was giving me a wonderfully stimulating blowing and the sound of that sucking filled the room.

Then all of a sudden the light came back on. The fellas (that were shielding us from view) were now gone. Quickly John pulled his mouth from my hard on. Now here I stood with my juiced up hard on, and fingers still giving me good anal vibes. Yet my surprise wasn't complete. The hot steam soon made itself felt on my relatively cool dick—having been in his mouth. It was the temperature change that got me to the point of no return. Then climax! Pow pow pow pow pow. I stood not knowing what to do. My hard on was bouncing with each spurt of cum and everyone saw me. I may even have ejaculated upon a straight fellow as sometimes I can shoot cum 4 feet or more.

When I finished climaxing I could begin to think. I didn't know what to do. I turned back my head to John and he sat there motionless. I saw that it was the fella to his right that still had his fingers in my ass.

Still unsure what to do, I decided to leave the steam room. I took my first step and my asshole moved off the fingers. No one said a word and I walked out with my saliva and cum wet hard on still standing up. The fellas stepped back and gavè me a straight path to the door and I disappeared. Thankfully no one complained but it was a climax I and maybe some straight fellas will never forget.

This was also before there was any substantial movement for gay rights and no sympathy or understanding of gay sexuality.

Can't Get Hard On for Mouth, But Can for Asshole.

I relaxed in the steam bath on a quiet weekday and wasn't sexually hot (unusual). I was just enjoying the steam until a nude stood fairly close to me. I was seated on the bench along the wall. Well, his side was facing me and I could see his genitals only a couple of feet away. I figured it was an opportune time, just to *look* at and visually *study* the guy's penis. It was a normal average soft penis. The foreskin wasn't covering the head so my eyes went back and forth from head to shaft.

I leaned forward to better see it and before I realized it my libido was encouraging me to "touch it, touch it." I brought my face close to it. He didn't pull away.

Now I realized I had a decision to make. I made it. Leaning forward, I opened my mouth. I used my tongue and lips to get half of the glans in my mouth. Then I sucked the full penis in. It didn't harden but I was enjoying just moving it in my mouth, etc.

In a minute the fellow gently pulled it from my mouth and went to shower. My new found appetite for cock still wasn't satisfied so I showered with him. I squatted down and sucked some more on it as he washed.

I followed him out of the shower and he walked around a bit. I still followed and every time he stopped I would bend over and take more sucks of it.

By now I was concerned that he wasn't getting a hard on. When he walked into the steam room again I went at his prick, doing my best to suck it up hard, to no avail. Then, a little later I asked "do you like it" (my blowing) and he said yes!

For a moment I was "lost." He asked me "do you fuck?" I said "yes."

We went back into the steam and I was all set to fuck him when he stepped behind me. His prick now pushed and probed for my hole. I reached back and guided the now well-stiffened penis to my hole. I felt it sliding between my ass cheeks and spreading my hole. At first I had one foot upon the bench but once he was firmly inside I then stood, bent forward. The fucking felt great but the steam was so hot we had to leave and go to a dressing room.

It felt great, the hard on sliding back into me, and I had to take it standing almost straight up as the room was very small. All I could do was to push out my ass toward his prick so I could get the entire thing into me. He gave me a fabulous lay and must have pressed and bumped my prostate as I was doing a slow cum. My semen and juices just ran slowly out.

After he came I pressed my ass toward him and kept his penis in me as long as possible. But as soon as he softened he slowly pulled out. The prick was soft yet still long and I missed it before it even came out!

After it fell from my hole I turned and asked "did you cum?" he nodded and we both smiled and went off to shower and go home our own ways.)×(

"SOME OLD FAG GAVE ME A COPY."

AUSTRALIA—Thanks for *Meat, Flesh, Sex,* and *Cum.* I found them all quite amazing reading. Even more amazing that I found them here in Australia at all.

Cum seemed to lose the pissy, cheesy, degrading flavour of the other three. Page 42 did turn me on—"Sucks Sailor's Scum from Youth's Butt-hole." What a perfect story. I really wish it was me there sucking that hot hole out and swallowing that juice. Also, the AMG boy opposite page 139. He would have to be my favourite jerk off idol from the days whey I was young, about 16. Some old fag gave me a copy of the AMG mag many years ago after he had sucked my dick. That boy was in there. Thanks for the memory—a Bob Hope line I believe.

Saw a little fuck angel in the street today. About 15 years old. Blond hair with come-to-bed eyes. He was leaning against the wall outside the Sunday paper offices. I took in the finger-lickin' bulge in his crotch and licked my lips at the way his full ass filled out the back of his tight white cords. Fuck, I could have got 2 years inside for what I was thinking. He must have noticed the way I was mentally undressing him because his eyes followed me all the way along the street. There was no way I was going to try anything with that piece of jail bait, as much as I would like to. I'll keep him in mind for jerk-off material tonight. The fantasy will no doubt be better than any reality, and without the danger.

Last night I got fucked by the biggest cock I have ever had, or even seen. Young guy, early twenties, slim. Uncut, which was heaven. I chewed his foreskin like a piece of gum, before and after he screwed me. It was tough getting it in but once it was there, oh brother! Just as well I had my little bottle of Amyl. While he was screwing he was biting my nipples real hard, which is my big weakness.

He shot up inside me and we both collapsed for awhile. Licking his huge cock clean afterwards was paradise. Just lately I really dig sucking cocks that have been inside my ass.

This all happened at the baths and afterwards I went into the orgy room, got down on my knees and within 20 minutes had about four loads of cum all over my face and chest while I forced two fingers up my tender hole.

Having lots of trouble at the baths here (do you still call them T rooms?). The cops have been regular visitors and quite a few friends have been bashed by frustrated hetero gangs. Once again there is talk of a gay vigilante group but I've heard those tales since I was 18 and nothing has been done as yet.

NEWS HAWK

by Boyd McDonald

Removing Elvis's Underpants

The Daily News ran that little UPI featurette about Elvis Presley's underpants being removed from a traveling exhibit and returned to the Presley museum in Memphis. Probably most papers did. It's a natural.

But the following day, July 28, the *News* ran another article, unsigned and uncredited, on Elvis's underpants. Whoever at the *News* is queer for Elvis's underpants turned up the additional information that the pair removed from the touring show was maroon briefs. Kathy Velvet, manager of the display, had them sent back to Memphis because they created too much attention and overwhelmed other items on display. Having enjoyed prolonged proximity to the star's dick, nuts, and butt, the maroon briefs naturally brought to mind—at least to the type of mind that produced the *News* article—Elvis's dick, nuts, and butt. He had a reputation for not being well hung but his butt, for most of his career, had an humiliating allure.

Imagine what would happen if the anonymous Jockey shorts fetishist at the *News* could see another item of Elvis's lingerie mentioned in *Elvis* by Albert Goldman: "thin white dancing briefs, no different really from a pair of women's panties . . ." Mmmmmmmm.

More Foreskins for Pennsylvania

"Standing in line in the supermarket," a Manhattan reader noticed an item in the July 22 *Weekly World News* that should have been on page one of the *Times*. "Blue Shield," says the tabloid, "plans to stop paying for circumcisions in Pennsylvania—claiming the controversial operations are unnecessary . . . a spokesman for the insurance group said there is 'no demonstrated health advantage to circumcision'." The paper did not mention that many men prefer foreskin. The reader comments, "Just think in twenty years . . ."

London Paper Runs
Photo of Boy's Butt

The *London Standard* ran a "large" photograph of a 13-year-old boy's "bruised bottom" which had been "caned" by a "grammar school headmaster," according to the July 26 *Economist*. A Manhattan publicist sent a xerox of the *Economist*; what I want now, and am trying to get from a correspondent in London, is a copy of the *Standard's* photo. My interest is twofold. Apart from the obvious one—the interest in bare butt that all healthy people have—I oppose butt-whipping, at least for such a trivial offense as that given in the *Economist* ("failing to get good marks in an exam"). I daresay the head-master who left his mark on the boy's butt still did not seriously reduce its natural beauty.

War Secret: Churchill Thought *Bachelor Mother* A Deanna Durbin Film

The absurd power that movies have over us can be seen in the fact that even an actress of Deanna Durbin's class (which is III) was discussed at the highest state levels during wartime. Sir Winston Churchill, according to a book review by John Gross in the July 29 *Times*, thought *Bachelor Mother* (1939) was a Durbin picture (it was a Ginger Rogers picture). Eric Ambler makes the startling revelation in *Here Lies*, the book under review. I say "startling" because it is startling that Sir Winston discussed, however inaccurately, such pictures as *Bachelor Mother* and such players as Deanna Durbin. Deanna did have talent but she was no Lynn Bari.

"This boy sure is hung"

A reader in Virginia writes, "I enjoy News Hawk more than any other feature." You'd think the editors could see it that way too, wouldn't you.

He enclosed the greatest news story I've ever seen, far greater than anything *The New York Times* has ever had.

Some background, supplied by the reader:

The place: Lexington, Virginia, "is about 5,000 pop. Stuffy *till now*. Home of Virginia Military Institute (Mmmmmmmm), Washington and Lee University, and the tombs of Robt. E. Lee and Stonewall Jackson."

The subject: Rockbridge County Commonwealth's Attorney Beverly C. "John" Read, "a Puritan and church pillar of the Jerry Falwell/Pat Robertson hue. Good family man, quote and unquote; community leader—the works. He was, supposedly, on his way up to the state legislature and perhaps thereafter to that shrine of statesmanship, the U.S. House of Representatives. Instead, now, he may be reduced to selling cars or insurance."

According to a magnificent article in the July 10 *Roanoke Times & World-News* by Mary Bishop and Tim Orwig, eight women gave testimony accusing the prosecutor of sexual misbehavior. "He has no right to sit in office and prosecute people," one of them said in summary. "He's just as much a criminal himself."

The article proves the value of print media. Television news men, most of whom probably have homosexual material in their memory, do not like to enact lines like "This boy sure is hung." Beverly made that evaluation of a month-old—repeat, month-old—boy in a photograph shown him by a woman client. Beverly asked the woman which side of the family the boy took after, a sneaky way of asking how the woman's husband was hung.

One woman testified that Beverly "would lean back in his recliner chair, rub himself through his pants and become sexually aroused."

"He'd say, 'This is what you do to me.' He was always stroking himself."

A woman who was pregnant when Beverly was her lawyer testified that "he asked her if she had milk in her breasts and whether they were firm or soft." The question was not germane to the litigation.

Another said he wanted "to perform oral sex on her," and "used common street terminology to describe the acts."

Another said "he had his hands on the back of my head and he was trying to get me" to perform oral sex. One woman testified that oral sex was "his favorite subject; several testified that "he asked them whether they had oral sex with their husbands or boyfriends." The chances are that Beverly, though a lawyer, did not use legal lingo like "oral sex;" the women testified that he used "vulgar language" and made "lewd suggestions."

Betty, Beverly's wife, was photographed with him at the trial. It is the strangest of matrimonial duties to "stand by your man" when he is accused of activities that are most un-matrimonial. John Ehrlichman's wife similarly appeared with him when he was on trial in the Watergate hearings but she divorced his ass when the hearings ended.

In Terms of Style

Peter Miller sent a clipping from the July 19 *Newsday* which bodes ill for the future of *The Village Voice's* style: its editor-in-chief, David Schneiderman, uses the phrase "in terms of." *Newsday* quotes Schneiderman as saying he fired the editor, Robert Friedman, "because things just didn't work out satisfactorily in terms of running the paper." Schneiderman is going to do Friedman's job "for an indefinite period." Whatever went wrong under Friedman, I don't believe he used, or permitted other writers and editors to use, "in terms of."

Love and Hate in Fort Worth

A reader in Fort Worth is "up to my ass in screaming preachers" and is appalled that the *Fort Worth Star-Telegram* devotes an entire section to religion. But the hateful preachers have been unable to subdue the city's secular life. For one thing, the reader has had three members of a motorcycle gang who take it in the ass. And he sent a clipping from the July 16 *Star-Telegram* which, he says, proves that there is "meaning to life" in the religion-crazed city. According to the article, "a screaming young woman" ran up to a police car. "She told us she had been robbed," Mike Culpepper, a cop, said. "She told us she was standing on a corner when a man riding a bicycle came up behind her and took her purse. She said he fired a gun and scared her and that she dropped her purse and he picked it up and rode away."

Culpepper saw the young man on a bicycle carrying a purse, chased him and caught him. The woman identified him as the thief. He said the woman had "approached him at the corner and made a sexual proposition . . . when he refused, she jumped on him and took his billfold and put it in her purse. He then drew his gun . . . and fired a round, and she dropped the purse and he picked it up and pedaled away."

Cops arrested both the man and the woman, charged both with robbery, and put both in jail. There, police discovered that the woman was a man.

In light of the fact that the cyclist rejected the sexual proposition from an apparent woman, if would be nice if he (the cyclist) rurned out to be gay. In that case, he would have rejected a proposition that he might have accepted had he known that it came from—don't you see?—another man.

Family Man

A Seattle reader sent a clipping from the July 10 *Post Intelligencer* which gives an insight into that symbol of reliability and respectability, the Family Man. A two-month-old baby boy awoke "early in the morning and started crying loudly and persistently." His father, Jimmie Lee Davenport, 27, sought to quiet him by socking him with his fist "at least twice." The baby died two days later of "skull fractures and head injuries."

Bad Days at Bad Axe

The attacks by bigots in rural Michigan on an isolated camp for women only, including lesbians, have been depicted here previously. A reader in Ft. Lauderdale has now sent another article on the conflict, this one by Thomas BeVier of the Knight-Ridder News Service, printed in the June 12 *Miami Herald,* which went to the trouble of illustrating it with a map showing the camp site 10 miles south of Bad Axe, characterized in the text as a "crop-growing, churchgoing town of 3,000."

BeVier's article, otherwise superb, does not raise the question of why the 3,000 residents of Bad Axe don't just grow their crops and go to their churches and let the women 10 miles away camp all they please. Nor does BeVier question the relevance of the remark made by one citizen of Bad Axe about the camp 10 miles to the south: "This goes against every grain of what we believe in." It is a radically un-American concept that if you don't "believe in" what's happening 10 miles, or 10 blocks, away from you, it must not be allowed to happen.

As in New York, where homosexuals are supported by the Episcopalians but attacked by the cracker Catholic cardinal and by a few equally bizarre rabbis in Brooklyn who are far out to the right of the Jewish religion, so in Bad Axe the local Episcopalian clergyman, The Reverend Mark Jenkins, supports the women and a holy roller, The Reverend James Willett of Faith Gospel Tabernacle, attacks them. Willett's remark that "There will be no weakness on our part" is the opposite of the truth. If heterosexuality were a strong impulse it wouldn't have to be enforced; if homosexuality were a slight one it wouldn't flourish as it does under attack.

But I do believe Sheriff Richard Stokan was right when he said, "I know that [the camp] is not something that is ever going to be welcomed with open arms." Open arms would mean the 3,000 crop-growing, churchgoing citizens of Bad Axe had gone gay.

Ari Was One

An important new addition to the roster of historic homosexuals is none other than Aristotle Onassis. Long before he married Jackie Kennedy, Ari had an affair with a young Turkish lieutenant, according to a new book, *Ari,* by Peter Evans (Summit Books; $19.95).

A reader in Atlanta alerted me with a clipping from the July 11 *Atlanta Journal* of an article about the book written by Ron Boyd of the *Dallas Times Herald.* I went out and bought the book. Ari's affair with the lieutenant is quickly disposed of in one terse sentence: "By tradition and temperament they became lovers." It's an unusually stingy treatment for a book of 367 pages, a book with page after page of "Acknowledgements" for everyone except the manufacturer of the author's toilet paper ("without which my anus . . ." *et cetera et cetera*). But looked at in another way, the author's casual, sophisticated dismissal of the fact that Ari had a gay sex affair is done in the tone of "Doesn't everyone, darling?"

Massaging Gene Raymond

"Clipper" from Brooklyn writes: "Saw your mention of Gene Raymond. I drooled for that guy long, long ago, when he was in a play on Broadway titled *Young Sinners*. He was then called Raymond Guion, before Hollywood. In one scene he is in a cabin in the woods being massaged by his trainer-companion. He is naked, lying on his stomach, just a towel over his ass. When he gets off the table, his towel is too-rapidly used to cover what would show if he were really naked. I saw the show a number of times, just to check."

Crime News

The June 30 *Newsweek* says former President Nixon once called Supreme Court Justice William Rehnquist a "clown." Any man who thinks Rehnquist is a clown can't be all bad.

The July 14 *People* reports "persistent rumors over the years about Roy Cohn's sexual preference." How nicely put; there are never rumors that a man is heterosexual.

The *Times* reports (July 12) that President Reagan wants to reduce the "already low" tax on profits from the sale of securities and other possessions. It is thus not completely true that Reagan is indifferent to the problems of minorities. There is one minority group he has always served well: millionaires.

Late Flashes

Georgia's ruinous drought is God's punishment for the state's anti "sodomy" law, according to Charley Shively, founder of *Fag Rag*, professor at the University of Massachusetts. Shively reached his conclusion by applying the principles of such fellow divines as Anita Bryant and the head of the Mormon church, who have blamed weather conditions on homosexuals, and also Jerry Falwell, who sees AIDS as God's punishment for homosexuality.

Shively believes that Georgians cannot obtain relief from the drought by praying for rain, but instead should pray that the Supreme Court will reverse its bizarre decision upholding the Georgia "sodomy" statute—the decision which, Shively says, drew forth the wrath of God.

A paper as stupid as *Weekly World News* has nothing to lose and can, to judge from a clipping sent by John Hansen of *Philadelphia Gay News*, be fun to read. The July 22 *Weekly World News* has another of those articles about Gadhafi wearing drag. The lead says he dresses like a "woman," paragraph seven that he dresses like a "lady." That the author, Rafe Klinger, can't make up his mind is understandable; the "top secret reports" and "high level sources" on which the article is based are vague in the extreme. Nor does Rafe inspire confidence by making three hyphenated words out of "nevertheless." Gadhafi isn't my beat, but any man who hates Reagan can't be all bad.

"I have recently cancelled my subscription," is the ominous beginning of a letter from a reader in Daly City, California. But the rest of the sentence is, ". . . to the San Mateo [California] *Times.*" He complained to the paper about its support of the Supreme Court anti-"sodomy" decision and got a two-page reply from one J. Hart Clinton containing proof beyond the shadow of a doubt that J. Hart, who is editor and publisher of the *Times*, is a cracker. J. Hart boasts that he went to Harvard Law School but he must have gotten his undergraduate degree at P.U. He couldn't have learned *this* at Harvard: "I have always been led to believe that our sexual organs were given to us for the purpose of procreating the race and not for the purpose of sheer pleasure." J. Hart gives a clue to his sordid background in the sentence, "When I was growing up, perverts were considered fair game for anyone to beat up." Thus it is not surprising that his letter should contain a hypothetical reference to killing his "wife in my bedroom." Note the use of "my," not "our." »«

39

"A LOT OF BOYS ARE
TOO IMPATIENT."

I boarded a bus to Montreal at Port Authority (Manhattan) about 10 in the evening.

The driver was a handsome, dapper man in his thirties looking trim in his uniform. He had the pleasantly jaded look that said I've seen it all; I've had it all.

I hadn't had sex in a week or two and the look of him roused me.

I found a seat at the back of the bus just north of the long rear seat and settled in for the long overnight ride. I had the seat to myself until we got to Binghamton. There two very pretty girls boarded and took the seat across the aisle. Just before take off an army of off duty drivers got on, making their way to the rear, filling the long seat, one sitting next to me. From Binghamton to Albany they filled the air with male talk, coming on to the girls, and it was pleasantly bawdy and roused me even more than I'd been. The drivers, while not in a class with the driver, were not bad and I don't think I'd have refused any of them.

From NYC to Binghamton and then across to Albany was a tortuous route and don't ask me why it was routed so, but it was so. At all the stops in between one or two drivers got out and when we finally hit Albany they were gone, along with a good many other passengers.

At Albany a husky young soldier made his way down the aisle, stopping at my seat. I was at the window and the other place was unoccupied. There were other seats by now and I can only think he stopped there because the pretty girls were still across the way.

He said, "Is anyone sitting here?" and I nodded no.

He was tall and broad-shouldered and effortlessly hoisted his duffle bag to the rack above us. He then removed his jacket and as he tossed it up there, his shirt underarms revealed a dampness nice to look at. He eased his robust frame into the seat next to me.

At the next stop, the girls departed. I feared he would now transfer his attractive bulk across the aisle. But he stayed where he was.

We began the small talk passengers make in such situations. He had just returned from two years in Germany, had two weeks leave, and was going to visit his family further upstate. He had to decide whether to re-enlist or apply to a college. He had spent his second year in Europe shacked up with a German girl and his girlfriend back home had gotten herself married.

The talk faded and he settled in his seat as did I. The conversation had been low-keyed even though I was as hot for this healthy young man as I've ever been for any boy. The pressures of the long ride, the example of the handsome driver, the bawdiness of the other drivers, the nearness of that healthy young body were building up. I cooled my head against my window and watched the passing lights. The young soldier was dozing and soon I feel asleep too.

When I woke up the soldier's leg was pressed sturdily against mine. Thinking he was still asleep, I returned the pressure, turning my body towards his. He was awake and his clear blue eyes gazed into mine with a message even clearer. I ran my hand along the muscular curve of that leg, coming to rest directly on my target. There was no longer a doubt. He was ready.

The bus was dark and quiet, the remaining passengers asleep or trying to sleep. I quickly unbuckled his pants, pulling out his prick as I worked. He was husky there too.

I fondled his balls for a few minutes. Then, with my hand on his calf for support, I lowered myself between his waiting legs and buried my head in his crotch.

We rode smoothly for the next few miles, my blow hole alternating smoothly between his balls and his dick. I then began blowing him seriously and without interruption until it started to spit. I then let up, allowing his juice to pour freely into and down my hole. When he was through, I dried him with my breath before returning his equipment to its resting place, rebuckling his pants and shifting my ass to the seat beside him.

We had exchanged no words during the operation and I once again rested my head against the cool window pane. He turned his back, prepared to go back to sleep. For me sleep was out and I stared once more at the lights outside, savoring the good taste of the young soldier's cream.

After about two hours I knew I wanted some more and decided to take the initiative. I ran my hand along the now familiar outline of his leg. Again he was awake and made no objection. I unbuckled his belt again. This time his dick was soft and I took it once again into my hole. It was sticky now. A little tongue work and it started to grow. I worked the entire crotch area now, the hairy part as well as the smooth. He responded but more slowly than before and it took several more miles than the first time.

I would have liked to visit the back region but hesitated to remove his pants. I contented myself with the undersides of his legs as far as I could reach and of course the balls.

My lips outlined the head of his prick and I spent about 15 minutes there. This was a blow job the way I like it; a lot of boys are too impatient, unless you have a second chance.

I made the most of it until the squirting started again. The second load was as healthy as the first and once again after drying him I put everything back in its proper place and resumed my seat. Not long afterward we arrived at his destination. He arose from his seat looking no worse for wear and hauled down his gear.

He didn't shake hands but did say thanks for a good trip. I said I enjoyed it and he sauntered up the aisle and out of the bus.

About an hour later I arrived in Montreal, no worse for wear. »«

FAG-BAITER SUCKS READER OFF.

Well, Boyd, you asked for it and here it is. Not a single sordid detail has been omitted. (I've changed the names.)

For ten years, all through the Seventies, I lived in the unheated attic of a rapidly deteriorating rooming house, located unfashionably close to the seedy downtown of a dying Midwestern city.

At the time I moved in, the other tenants were all either college students or young working people like myself. Before too long, however, they'd all been replaced by unemployed alcoholics. The bad drove out the good, but I stayed on.

In the room directly below my own, there lived a fellow whom I'll call Bill. He was mentally disturbed. In the middle of the night I would hear him screaming "I WANNA GET FUCKED!" Finally I went to him, told him I was gay, and offered to service him, if he was really as desperate as all that. On numerous occasions I tried to suck him off, but his cock, though large and heavy, could never achieve a full erection. He claimed that this was because he'd been an alcoholic since long before puberty.

Bill not only had a limp dick; he also had a loose tongue. He described our strenuous, yet unsuccessful, sessions to the drunkard who lived in the apartment next door to his own. This gentleman, whom I'll call Harry, was a homophobe. Indeed, he made sneering remarks practically every time he encountered me in the hallway or on the stairs.

I should have known what this meant: that he was secretly, lustfully fascinated by the very acts which he seemed so ardently to despise.

But I didn't catch on till the following Christmas Day when, the building half empty, he finally summoned up the courage to come tapping at my door. When I asked him what I could do for him, he said he wanted to know what sort of intimacies Bill and I had shared. I could tell right away, just from the tone of his voice, that he was horny as hell. That was O.K. by me. I was game to take him on.

"I sucked his cock," I replied, "but I was never able to make him come." I used as provocative a tone as I could manage. So then Harry, of all people, invited me down to his nice, warm apartment to suck *my* cock.

43

Grabbing a tube of lubricant and a roll of toilet paper, I hurried downstairs before he could change his mind.

I should mention that, whereas Bill was of average appearance, Harry was downright unattractive. He looked sort of like Hitler, except without that funny little moustache. Furthermore, year after year of guzzling beer had left him with an obscenely protruding pot belly which seemed all the more pronounced when he undressed.

But what the heck, it was Christmas and I wanted us both to have a good time.

Once in his room, with the door safely locked, I performed as sensuous a striptease as I could under the circumstances. I only regretted that I hadn't more clothes to take off. He leered with anticipation. I reclined on his bed. With surprising enthusiasm, he commenced to gobble my dork. His lips and tongue were remarkably busy. I moaned with pleasure. It felt so good, I asked him to stop because I knew if I let him continue much longer I was going to shoot my load. Rather selfishly, I'd already made up my mind that I was going to see his cream before I squirted my own.

"I came, bucking and rearing and thrashing all over the bed."

So we exchanged places and I began to give him a hand job. His cock was fat and stubby, smaller than Bill's, but at least it was hard. A low groan was the only warning he gave as his orgasm approached. His jiz was far from copious. I was not impressed.

At this point I harbored fears that his interest might lag. Not so, however, "Now it's your turn," he huskily intoned. And so I lay back and let his energetic fingers do their stuff. When I came, I really put on a show, bucking and rearing and thrashing all over the bed. I shrieked his name as I fired the first volley. He didn't appreciate that. I suppose he was fretting that Bill might overhear.

Upon my arrival home from the work the following evening, Harry drunkenly confronted me in the hallway. Making threats that were vaguely connected with our jerk-off session of the night before, he managed to shake me down for a couple of bucks. It was an ugly scene. When inebriated, he was like a raging demon let loose upon the land.

The following day, having sobered up, he was somewhat apologetic. He even offered to give me back my money. Furthermore, he promised he would never again try to blackmail me. And then he confessed that, during his early adolescence, he and a neighbor boy used to camp out together in each other's backyards; in the privacy of the tent they shared, they would butt-fuck the night away.

I must admit it stimulated me quite pleasantly to envision such a pair of apparently wholesome, outdoorsy young lads engaged in that kind of covert naughtiness. And I was more than a little amused to consider the fact that this man who for weeks had been scornfully calling me a "percy" had, at a tender age, accustomed himself to a mode of homosexual intercourse which I had yet to experience.

Approximately a month passed by before Harry came knocking at my door again. He thought there was a mouse at large in his closet and wanted me to help catch it. I consented, though I figured (rightly) that it would prove to be a wild goose chase.

And so I emptied his closet of all its contents while he stood poised with a broom, ready to crush any rodent that might emerge. He seemed utterly terrified. I of course maintained my cool, thereby garnering at least a nominal measure of his respect.

After all his debris had been returned to its place, he engaged me in conversation. He complained that he was short of cash. I offered to loan him five bucks. As I handed him the bill, I noticed a lecherous smile flicker across his face. Instinctively, I knew what had just passed through his mind. "I don't suppose you'd care to earn this money," I said seductively.

He seemed uncertain. To help him make up his mind, I briefly returned to my room, fetching a picture book by Tom of Finland. This was a tactical error on my part; for the next quarter hour I had to fend off his ardent attempts to sodomize me.

Finally, and not very graciously, he gave up. At this point he commenced to complain of an irritating back pain. I offered to give him a rubdown. He took me up on this, instructing me to work my way progressively lower along his spine.

Cocksucker Jailed For Raping Woman.

Finally, he asked me to massage his naked butt. I should've guessed what was next on the agenda. Suddenly, unexpectedly, he turned over on his back and there it was: his cock, proud, stiff, and hard.

I didn't waste any time asking permission. Without a by-your-leave, my lips and tongue went to work. Harry groaned with pleasure as my mouth encompassed his dick totally. It felt like a huge hunk of hard candy and I treated it accordingly. It smelled and tasted clean (thank goodness). I worked hard; I chafed my lips till they were numb; afterward they sported a rosy glow.

He requested that I simultaneously suck and jack him off. This perplexed me at first, but I soon fell into the rhythm of the procedure.

Then he started to fret. "What if it comes?" he said, rather quaintly.

My mouth being otherwise engaged, all I could do was try to murmur reassuringly.

His tension approaching the breaking point, he continued thusly: "I think it's gonna come . . . Yeah . . . it's coming . . . here it comes . . . Unnnggh!"

He bucked and reared a bit. Otherwise I noticed nothing. I neither felt nor tasted anything discernible. Like Bill, he'd been a boozer far too long; all he had left was his lust, without any wherewithall to back it up.

Afterward I didn't feel sick or nauseated or ashamed or guilty or dirty or anything in particular, even though this was the first time anyone had ever come in my mouth.

Harry was amazed. He looked at me as though I had just taken poison. "Didn't it bother you, swallowing that stuff?"

"It was delicious," I crooned contentedly, astounding him all the more.

He seemed to have found my efforts satisfying. I asked him, "Did you like it better when I went fast or when I went slow?"

"Both," he replied without hesitation and almost distractedly.

He gave me a good hand job. He seemed to find the size of my erection impressive; he exclaimed when I undressed. For a change, he was gentle.

I climaxed readily, squealing with joy even as he exhorted me to keep the noise to a minimum.

Soon after that, I moved to a different part of town. Consequently, I didn't see much of Harry anymore. A couple years ago, however, I noticed his name in the newspaper: he'd been sent to prison for raping a woman.

It seemed incredible that a cock I sucked could be capable of committing such a different type of act. »«

"I LOOKED UP AT HIS FACE."

When I turned 24 last year I began to realize that my trim and defined body would not stay that way unless I put a little effort into maintaining it. I decided it was time for a gym; but where to go?

I was apartment sitting in Brooklyn for some friends who were vacationing and would pass an all black health spa coming to and from the subway each afternoon. I, being very white and very blond, contemplated going inside several times but just wasn't sure how everyone in the gym would feel about me. As it turned out, I signed up for several months of "rigorous working out" and was quite happy I did.

Each day I worked out I would tell myself *not* to stare, for this would surely get me into trouble. I was surrounded by enormous black men. Tight asses, huge dicks, chests, arms, and legs all around me (at times I thought I had died and gone to heaven).

One day I just couldn't help myself, for in walked Jerry; a vision. As I was on my back, struggling to finish by 50 situps, Jerry (I got his name from a large gold plate he wore around his neck) was doing an exercise nearby. He was lifting himself up and down on this handlebar type apparatus. He had the roundest ass I had ever seen. His legs were thick and you could see every muscle in them.

He eventually reversed his position and was now facing me. I thought for sure he saw me checking out the tip of his big dick, which was not coming out from his shorts, so I quickly turned away.

After about an hour of working out, Jerry headed for the showers, and I (dubiously, of course) followed. We were in the locker room when I first saw him completely naked. His back was to me and when he bent over to remove his socks I felt like jumping across the room and biting that hard ass of his. My heart was pounding. I could not believe that not only did I get to see him naked, but that I was now about to take a shower with him.

We both entered the shower, which was one large stall with four shower heads. I waited until I caught a glimpse of him putting his face to the water, because I knew that would be when I could stare all I wanted to without him catching me.

After awhile I just didn't care. I got to see his cock. I wasn't exactly sure (especially because it was so big already, just hanging there soft) but it seemed to be getting bigger.

Yes, it was. This fucking guy's dick was getting bigger than I imagined it would be—and in the same shower as *me*.

I figured it would be O.K. to do something. But there was still a bit of uncertainty on my part. I reached over to borrow the soap he was holding and just started to soap his cock. Just then another guy entered the bathroom and we had to cool it for awhile.

After the other guy left, I thought we would resume what we (I) had started but Jerry turned off his water and went back into the locker room. I thought, "Shit. The guy's nervous now and we'll *never* finish up."

I followed him back to the locker room and watched as he began dressing. I thought that maybe he would change his mind and we would start in again, but no.

I decided to begin putting on my clothes as well, being that Jerry was now fully dressed and seemed to be ready to walk out the door. I was sitting on one of those small dressing benches putting on my socks when I saw two feet standing in front of me. As I panned up the legs I saw that it was Jerry, and in his hands was that huge, beautiful cock he had teased me with in the shower.

My mouth immediately just opened up. He stood on tip toes to make sure the *entire* thing went all the way down my throat.

I couldn't believe that his cock went all the way down (even though I *do* give great head, I was not aware that my throat was ready for such circumferences). I looked up at his face as he began to fuck my mouth. As he was about to come he closed his eyes and began to talk to me, calling me baby.

I was beating my own big dick and his words alone made me shoot. He went crazy at the sight of me cumming and shot a big hot load down my throat.)«(

I PULLED IT OUT.

While collecting a few cans in Centrel Park, I saw this thin fairly clean looking man about in his fiftys siting [*sic*] on a bench. He had two shopping bags next to him filled with some clothes. He was watching me so I sat on the next bench from him. He was still looking at me. I was wearing blue shorts and tank top on my thin hairless body. (Thanks to Neet.) I also carry a small back pack that I keep everything in. House keys and money. Nothing in my pockets.

He came over and asked me the time. He then asked me if I might have some wine in my pack, that he was out of work and was sleeping in the park. I told him if he wanted a bottle of wine I would give him the money and that I didn't drink anymore. But first he would have to suck me off. That when I came he would have to taste all my cum and not spit it out but swallow it after tasting it for a few minutes.

He told me he never did that, that I should get my self a women.

48

I told him a women cant suck a cock as good as a man. The only thing they do is spread there legs.

I got up and was ready to leave when he said okey. I told him first the blow job and then I would give the money for his wine.

We went into the woods where nobody could see us. I carry a bath towel in my pack that I laid on the grass after taking off all my clothes except my shoes. He watched me while I undressed. He was licking his lips. I already had a hard on, 6 inches hard, hard and uncut. I hadn't had any sex or did I jack off in a week. So I knew there was plenty of cum in my balls.

I laid on the towel and he started sucking my cock. I told him to go faster. I put my hands on the back of his head and pressed it down. I started fucking him in the mouth. My whole cock was going into his mouth now. I shot a heavy wad into his mouth. Some of it began dripping out.

I asked him if he liked the taste. He didn't answer. I got dressed and gave him the money he needed.

About two hours later I was siting on the same bench where I met him the first time. I saw him again. He came over and sat down next to me with his two shoping bags. I asked him if he got his wine. He said he got a pt. of Thunderbird. He did look a little drunk.

He then asked me if he could do it again. I told him I didn't have any more money, only cans. He said he didn't want money. We went to the same spot. This time I didn't have to tell him to go faster. He tool the whole cock into his mouth, started playing with my balls and rubbing and feeling my behind and theighs. I shot a wad into his mouth. I got dressed and went home.

There was this old man lying on this bench. He looked like he had the shakes. I sat down next to where he was lying and took out a bottle of Scotch that was about 1/3 full that I found in the park while collecting cans. When he saw the bottle he sat up and asked me if he could have a taste. I said he could have the whole bottle. But first he would have to taste my cum.

He asked me what I meant.

I said, "You have to suck my cock." He said no. So I got up an started walking into the woods. He began following me. When I found a good spot I took the towel out of my pack and took my clothes off.

This time I just put my shorts and pack on the towel so they would't get dirty. I stood up and he squated down in front of my cock. I stuck my cock into his mouth. I had half a hard on. It began getting harder and he started choking so I pulled it out. I told him I would go easy.

49

"He was jacking me off while sucking my hole."

He asked me if he could have a little drink. I let him have a little bit. I had a full hard on now. I told him to jack me off and then I put it back into his mouth. I fucked him in the mouth slowing and then I began coming. He began gaging, choking. He never did it before. I gave him the rest of the Scotch and he left.

While siting in the neighborhood library, not reading, an elderly gentleman dressed in a suit, not bad looking for his age, a little pot belley, was staring at my hairless slim legs. When I saw him, I put my hand between my legs and started rubing my cock and balls. I was wearing loose shorts.

He came over and said, "Hi can I buy you a cup of coffee."

I said "okey."

When we got outside he asked me where I lived. I told him I lived with my sister (not true). I told him we could go to his place.

He said I was very direct. He took me to his small apt., a room with kitchen & bath. I sat on his bed and began taking my clothes off. I told him I didn't want any coffee.

He came over. He kept his clothes on. All he took off was his jacket and tie.

He started kissing me. I told him I dont kiss. He started licking my neck & chest, working his way down to my cock & balls and started fingering my ass.

He said you never got fucked in the ass have you, its like a pea hole.

When he said this he raised my legs, slid a pillow under my back to raise my ass, and began sucking my hole. It felt so good that I felt like shiting in his mouth. He was jacking me off while sucking my hole.

I then told him I was cuming. He put my cock into his mouth. I shot a few wads. He swallowed all of it.

There's an old man that sits and reads his newspaper, usually on the same bench every morning when the weather's nice. There's a highway a short distance down a low hill from where he sits. Between the bench and highway there are a lot of trees and bushes. You can hardly see the highway. There's a low iron fence that anyone can step over in front of the bench.

So one morning I saw him siting there. I steped over the fence a short distance away and walked along one of the narrow paths until I was close to where he was siting, about 15 ft. I was wearing shorts and a hooded sweat shirt. I just took my shorts off. I had some cans and bottles that I collected and shook the bag a little so he would hear it. He did, because he got up and looked down over the fence and saw me. My back was facing him so he could see my hairless legs & behind only.

I began jacking off. He thought I didnt see him. I turned around. I had a hard on. He lean over the fence for a closer look. I started beating my meat faster.

I turned around again. He could see my exposed ass. He steped over the fence. I started cuming and faced him so he could see the cum squirting out of my cock. He thought I didn't see him. I put my shorts on and took off.

A few days later I saw him and let him see me step over the fence. I went into the bushes, began taking off my shorts, and started jacking off. I left my hooded sweat shirt on. I could see he was coming down so I continued jacking off.

He came over to where I was and asked me if he could watch. He said his wife was sick, that they dont have sex.

I asked him if he wanted to jack me off. He said he like to suck me off. He took all my cum and swallowed it.

Early one morning the Building where I live I took the Elevator down to the Basement to pick up some cans that someone had for me. It was too early. The door was locked where the cans were kept and nobody was there to open it yet.

So walking back to the Elevator I saw this guy doing his laundry. So I walked into the Laundry Room and sat in this one chair they have. I was wearing shorts and T shirt.

He looked at me and I told him I was waiting for some cans somebody had for me. I told him it was too early that nobody was there to open the door.

He said nobody comes down here this early. I began rubing between my legs. He began breathing heavy and his lips were parted. I stood up and took my shorts off. He came over and told me to sit down.

He then knelt between my legs and started sucking me off. It only took a couple of minutes and I cum. He tasted it and then spit it into a sink.

He asked me if I could piss into his mouth before any body came, so after my cock got soft I pissed into his mouth. He drank some of it. Some wet the floor. He wipe it up.

For the past few years Ive been going to the parks, even before I started collecting cans and riding my bike, Ive sucked and been sucked off dozens of times. I've had big men with small cocks and small men with large cocks and sometimes the opposite. Ive had older men with hard cocks and there balls were full of cum and there were younger men that could only get half a hard on and a few drips of cum. But sometimes it would be the opposite.

51

BUS DRIVER SUCKS RIDER'S BUTT.

Six o'clock in the morning after an all-night ride from New York City I arrive at a bus terminal in Montreal. Another four hours before my bus to Ottawa. I am not familiar with the beautiful city and as I enter the building the surroundings look dismal. I have no idea where at this hour to go sightseeing.

Inside the station was barren except for a weary traveler here and there. The driver of the bus I'd been on came in a few minutes later and disappeared into the dispatcher's office. He had heightened my trip with his looks: dapper, about 35, compact, and rakish with his cap at an angle, highlighting black curly hair, a dimple, a cleft chin, and the expression of a man who had been everywhere.

I had been fortunate on the trip in a more immediate way by having as a seat mate a lusty young soldier who was as willing to enjoy my company as I was his, and I sucked him off twice.

But now it's six o'clock and four hours to be killed. I put my bag in a locker and entered the men's room of necessity. It was clean and empty of patrons. I approached a urinal and prepared to do what I had to do. The door swung open and there was the handsome driver, who approached another urinal to do what he had to do.

He nodded in recognition and matter of factly whipped out his cock (no other word will describe it). I thought, as I so often have, when you've got that you've got it all. It complemented the muscular body in the trim uniform, the Eisenhower jacket showing off the lean but well rounded ass. Up this close he looked disheveled from the trip with a suggestion of beard molding the firm chin.

He said something about the long trip and this enabled me to continue to check him out as I responded in agreement.

We were both pissing heavily by now and as the conversation continued it was proper to look his way. The cock itself was long and hooded.

I finished my leak first and put my dick away. The continuing exchanges on travel allowed me to stay and watch while he uncovered his from the head and ridded himself of the last few drops. I went to one of the basins, washed my hands, and left him to himself.

Back in the waiting room nothing had changed. The restaurant was closed so I walked over to a vending machine along the wall and bought me a container of weak-looking coffee and took a seat. The interlude in the men's room had been pleasant but I still had a lot of time to kill.

A few minutes later the driver emerged and as he passed me he glanced at the paper cup.

"Hey, that shit'll kill you."

52

I shrugged.

"You catching the next bus to Ottawa?"

I nodded.

"That's a long time," he said. He offered to give me some fresh coffee at his pad "a few blocks from here," plus "maybe some breakfast." Did I imagine it or was there a slight pause between the last two words? Anyway, I agreed and we went to the parking lot to his car. We drove to his place, a small studio apartment which had the same lived-in look that he did.

He put on some coffee and while it was brewing he began to undress with the same self-assured matter-of-factness with which he had pulled out his cock in the men's room. He stripped down to his underpants and sat on his bed while I sat in a straight-up chair opposite.

He led off the conversation with more of the same directness. "So, how was the trip?"

I said it was not as bad as I expected.

"How was the soldier?"

This surprised me. I had made out with my seat mate but I'd thought we'd been discreet.

"Pretty good," I stammered. "How the hell did you know?"

He laughed. "I didn't *know*, I just figured. I thought when you got on that you'd probably make it with one of the boys in the back."

He was referring to a bunch of drivers who rode part way on the way to their homes. I explained that they had been busy with a couple of good-looking girls opposite me for one thing and that I wasn't about to come on to five guys, for another.

"If the girls weren't there, they might have come on to you," he said. "I don't know a single driver on a long distance route who won't settle for a man if there is nothing else around."

"Same as you?" I asked.

"Oh, now, I'm different. I'll settle for a broad if there's nothing else around. Don't tell anybody, but I like guys. Guys with full, soft lips. It's what I noticed about you when you came aboard."

He slipped out of his underpants and stood up and it was easy to see why the uniform had fit so well. Broad of neck, shoulders, and chest, flat below, and that cock! Muscular of arms and legs, he could have stepped from the pages of a beef cake magazine, except maybe for one thing: he was hairy. Not inordinately, but the well-made chest was matted with the same black curly hair that crowned his head and encircled his crotch. It tapered as it approached the flat belly, then narrowed to an arrow-like line pointing toward his tool house. Arms, legs, and backside were free of what some regard as a blemish. I am no hair fetishist but to these eyes he remained as he had when fully clothed—a fucking beauty.

He came over to where I was sitting, repeating "guys with full soft lips" as he rubbed his cock against my mouth. After a few minutes I stuck out my tongue, using it to roll back the hood and lick the immense head underneath.

He pushed his cock in further and said, "Hey, why don't you get out of those clothes. You got plenty of time."

I stripped and he commented, "Nice ass. Great legs."

He stretched out on the bed and said. "Come on over and get comfortable."

Over there I lowered my head and began to suck but he pulled out, saying, "Hey, let me dip it in shit first. It'll taste much better later."

I turned over and he straddled me, working his cock into my butt-hole. He knew how, all right, and as the hairy torso tickled my back, he began to ride me as though we'd done it many times before.

After he came and pulled out he rolled over on his back, saying, "When you go down next time it'll really taste good."

He set the alarm so I wouldn't miss my bus and we took a nap. When the alarm went off I still had an hour and we were soon at it again. Again, with matter-of-factness that was as refreshing as anything about him, he arranged our positions.

"I'm something of a cunt lapper you know," he said, and began to kiss my ass gently until he was eating my pussy. He had maneuvered us into sort of a 69 set up and I was able to suck his cock.

And he was right, it tasted a lot better cum-crusted and with the aroma of my asshole.

I sucked and sucked while he continued to feed on my box. He came again heavy and creamy and I lapped it up. One of the better breakfasts I've had.

It was time to go. We showered and dressed and he drove me back to the terminal, promising to get together on my return in two days, if possible.

I boarded the bus to Ottawa, somehow not at all tired.)«(

"HE HAD A FABULOUS BODY"

Greetings from the snow covered hills of West Virginia. Today it is snowing and it reminds me of what I used to do when I was in my early 20s. I was out walking around in the woods behind the house one snowy night and I got so horny that I stripped off all my clothes and stood there with the snow falling on me and jacked off. I was so hot the cold wind didn't chill me. It was so peaceful and quiet in those days with nothing but the snowflakes falling on me. When I was ready to come I laid down and buried my cock in the snow and shot my load. It was really a terrific blast off. I got up and put my clothes back on but I was beginning to get cold before I was dressed.

Needless to say I repeated that performance a lot more times when conditions were right.

Due to the AIDS scare (yes AIDS have come to West Virginia) I have quit my active sex life so I'll write to you of some of my experiences of long ago.

I had a friend (he is dead now from a heart attack) and we would meet and go on to Parkersburg. He would drive my car and while we were driving the 30 miles up there, I would be down on him sucking his cock most of the way. He would shoot his load before we got there. It was a little uncomfortable position to be in to suck but I really enjoyed it. The movement of the car would help his hard cock to move in and out of my mouth. I would take it all the way down to the root the way he liked it and then the car movement would move it enough to keep it throbbing.

He wanted to go with me as he liked to watch me suck other men's cocks. Sometimes we would hit it lucky and he would get to watch me suck two or three in the rest room at the bus terminal or at a roadside park above town.

Then on our way home I would go down on him again. Sometimes he would drive slow and I would get two loads from him.

One night I hadn't got him off going up and I should have as it turned out. We picked up this 20-year-old stud at the bus station and he went out in the car with us to a parking place he knew in a secluded spot. The young stud undressed and he had a fabulous body and nice eight-inch cock. Don got to watch me lick him all over. We threw a blanket down to lie on. I sucked his balls and sucked all his cock in and Don enjoyed watching me eat out his ass. Don got so hot watching me get the young stud off that he had to fuck me in the ass then and there. We undressed completely and threw our clothes on the hood of the car and were were so busy in what we were doing that the pick-up slipped my bill fold out of my pocket and removed the money (some twelve dollars) and we didn't even know it. I was robbed right before my eyes. I of course didn't miss the money until I got home.

We were supposed to meet him again the next week and he was going to bring his brother along, but needless to say I didn't go back.

Here is another one about a man with a very sensitive asshole. I picked up this 40-year-old at my favorite roadside park above town. He was driving a four wheel drive vehicle and he said we would take it and out to a secluded place. It's a good thing he did because when my tongue would hit his asshole he would yell for joy so loud anyone in a mile would have heard him. He was a nice looking small man with about a six inch cock. He would completely undress and get in the back of his vehicle and lie down and I would start to work on him. I sucked and sucked on his cock and it just got semi hard. I then went to sucking his nuts and then I started licking back between his legs and he got to getting harder and when my tongue hit the soft pussy-like asshole he hardened up and started to moan and yell. I had found the secret to his pleasure.

I spent a long time on his ass, licking the cheeks and licking up the crack and then burying my tongue in his hole as far as I could. I would then go back to his now hard cock and suck on it and when I wanted to finish him off I would take my finger and play with his asshole and he would start spurting.

A friend of mine that knew him said that his wife had boy friends and I of course guessed why as he couldn't get it hard enough to put it to her without some ass play. She later divored him but I lost track of him.

Here is an in depth interview that I gave myself. Excuse the typing as I am out of practice and also my typewriter is getting old, like I am. It is hard to make enough money to live on anymore *honestly*. I draw my Social Security and work too and then couldn't live if I didn't live in the country where I raise my groveries in the summer and no rent to pay (just taxes).

What age partner do you like best? I like a man between 25 and 35 or 40 the best as they are old enough to know what they want. They have the hottest and hardest cocks. I preferred them married as I can give them what their wives can't or won't give them.

What action do you prefer? I of course like to suck his cock the best. An uncut one so I can get cock cheese or at least the lingering odor of it. Then I like to suck his nipples. Then comes his asshole in third place and then his balls to lightly lick on and take in my mouth one at a time and if possible both at once to roll around my mouth. Then I like to suck his toes. I like to take each toe in my mouth and suck on them and then get as much of his whole foot as I can in my mouth. Then I like to lick his armpits if he hasn't used deodorants. I don't want no aftershave lotion or perfumes on his body. I want the natural smells of a man. I like to lick around his balls when he hasn't bathed for a day and has the odor of piss in the hairs of his crotch. The same goes for the odors around his asshole and of course his toes. Most people bathe too often

Do you like the taste of cum? I love the taste of cum except you do get some that is bitter. Some of it has the taste of beer if they have drank too much but that doesn't hurt it, but I prefer the natural taste of cum. I love the smell of it, too.

What is the biggest cock you ever had? Eleven inches is the biggest one I have ever measured. It of course was too big to do much sucking on. I had one bigger one time at a roadside park. I should have asked him how big it was. It must have been 12 inches and it was so big around. It was as big around as my arm and that would be seven inches. The big red head was all I could get in my mouth but he got off with me just licking it and sucking on it and licking his piss hole. I would hold his cock and spread open the piss hole and then lick inside it. His cock was lovely to see. I wasn't into piss much at that time but that would have been a wonderful experience to drink piss from that monster and to lie underneath him and watch the golden piss streaming out of that big pee hole, coming down and hitting and warming my whole body and face.

When did you first get into piss? I was 41 when I had my first drink of piss. I thought I would try it and it was so good I kept it up. It was really good tasting and to feel that war piss spurting against your tongue and roof of your mouth was a turn on. I was lucky that his piss was so good as of course some of it is bitter. I prefer the strong and bitter to beer piss, but any of it is good. With beer piss you get more of course. I can drink down all a stud can give me without spilling a drop.

Does everybody that you ask for piss give it to you? No, not eveybody, but most of them. I enjoy watching for the reaction when asking them. Some have a surprised look on their face. I have had a lot that it was the first time they had ever done it. Some will get a hard on while they are doing it. I like to get their piss really before I suck them off as they are really hotter after doing it. I have got some that were experienced pissers. One boy I can remember really gave a wonderful shower. I got out of the car and knelt down in front of him as though I was tying my shoe and he took out his cock and started pissing in my face, in my mouth, in my ears and hair and it was running down all over me, and he gave me a lot too. I went home that night smelling good and I had a good taste in my mouth all the way home.

Did you ever drink your own piss? Yes. I lie down on my back and position my pisser in a position so that I can watch it come out and hit my mouth and drink it down. I also will piss in a glass and drink it down. I had a friend that preferred to piss in a glass and drink his own, but to have someone watch him do it. I also like to piss my pants. I will be coming home in the car and I just start pissing and that warm piss really feels good coming out between your legs and spreading all around your crotch. Your jeans also smell good the next day.

Describe how you beat your meat. I usually beat off every two or three days. Sometimes oftener. I will always beat my meat when I have been out cruising and come home. I like to get in the nude and lie in bed and think back on the cocks I've had, but mostly of the one I let get away. I start out with playing with my nipples and thinking of what could have happened, what I would have done to him, what he would have been like, and my cock starts getting hard without my touching it. I then start stroking my cock and skinning the foreskin back. Then I go back up to my sensitive nipples and play with them while I watch my cock throbbing and a little pre-cum comes out the pee hole which I then take and spread over the head. I will now take my nuts in hand and caress them. I like to make it last a half hour. If I let it go a half hour I will have a lot bigger load of cum worked up to shoot. It will shoot as far as my nipples for the first spurt, but most of it lands around my cock hairs. I scoop it all up and eat it. It's very good tasting. I still shoot a big load but not as much as I did 20 and 30 years ago. Everybody always remarks about how much I shoot.

Do you like to jack off other men? Yes. I like to see it shoot out and to be lying where it can hit me in the face.

Do you like for other men to suck you off? Yes I do, but I have only five inches and not everybody will suck a cock that small. But that is really a perfect size for sucking. I like to suck a cock that size, as it's so much easier to suck. I always like to get the whole cock in my mouth and feel their cock hairs against my lips and sometimes that is quite a job with one too big.

What is the biggest cock you have ever had all the way in? Ten inches. I kept working on that big cock and sliding more and more in and I finally got so hot that my throat opened up and the whole ten inches slid in where I could work my throat muscles on it. The stud looked down when he seen it disappear and said, "Well you took the whole thing, you are the second person to do so."

Do you like to be fucked in the ass? At times, if the man knows how to do it. I have a friend with a five incher that just works right for fucking my ass and he really makes me feel wonderful. I like it in a long time. The bigger the cock the longer I like in it. Most of them shoot off before I really get used to the feel of it in my ass. I like to be able to feel it shoot in my ass. I had one guy that was an expert at fucking and he would take it slow and let it lie in my ass without moving for a long time and then when he did fuck and shoot I could feel every drop of his cum hit my insides. He would then let his dick lie there and piss up my ass.

Would you say your sex life has been satisfactory? Yes. I started at 17 and for 47 years have done what came naturally. Sex between men is natural but men are brainwashed into thinking they are supposed to have sex with women. Women have also been brainwashed into thinking they are supposed to have children. You can notice not many women can stand this kind or life and they want to get out of the home to work. »«

"I WENT STRAIGHT TO MY KNEES."

SAN FRANCISCO–I know a guy named Charles who was born and raised in a suburb of London. He's had a modest success with a rock band in these parts. He comes from a comfortable middle-class background and he spent most of his formative years in swank private schools.

He wrote a love song entitled "You Smiled and I Knew." I asked him whose smile had inspired the lyrics and he told me that he'd met a young guy named Li, whose parents were Greek and Vietnamese, and who had a smile that was "utterly captivating." Charles was playing a gig with his band and Li came up to him during a break to ask for his autograph. "When he held out the paper and pen to me," Charles wrote, "I was just stunned by his smile. His face was beautiful, to begin with, but when he smiled it was—well, as I said: overpowering."

Charles, by the way, is lean, with rather aquiline features, large grey-green eyes, and light brown hair. Li, as Charles described him, was small and boyish, with an appearance that was delicate and appealing. Charles wrote, "From the moment I saw him, I was determined to have him naked in my arms. It's difficult to explain, but I could tell every contour of his body, just from seeing his face. I knew exactly the look of his cock and balls and I knew that he had delicious come."

Charles had to be back on stage and asked Li to come back after the end of the show. "He went out and spent the rest of the evening looking up at me with that astonishing smile," Charles wrote, "and I had a deuce of a time to keep from making a fool of myself."

When the job was over, Charles went to his dressing room, hot and sweaty. Li appeared at the door a few minutes later. "When he came in," Charles wrote, "I was nearly speechless. He was so damned attractive. Without saying a word, I closed the door and locked it and I turned to him and held out my arms. He came to me and we embraced and kissed eagerly. I was so thrilled I could scarcely breathe. I felt his crotch and his cock was hard, as mine was. When I began taking my clothes off, Li looked at the door and asked if it was safe. I said it was and in just a few more minutes Li and I were naked. When he saw my cock, he said, "So *big!*" It isn't really all that big but it's twice the size of his, which was precisely as I'd imagined it. I went straight to my knees and took it all into my mouth. Li let out a whine and his whole body shook and he shot his cum—delicious, musky stuff, it was; and I was just in heaven."

"HE REALLY KNEW HOW TO GET SUCKED."

In your letter you say that it is inspiring that I have several hundred cocksucking experiences to report. Most of those experiences were unremarkable and not worth mentioning. Only a handful, perhaps two dozen, are worth writing about.

You made one comment in your letter which I must agree with. You said, "The simple truth is more pornographic than pornography, which lacks credibility." You are so right. A good example of this is the magazine *First Hand* (when edited by Brandon Judell). It became more pornographic until the magazine lost all its appeal.

I may not be exactly the type of writer that you like; I don't like foreskins, body odors, scat, urine, dangerous situations, smelly underwear, etc. I know it sounds boring but you must have some readers who like my kind of sex.

I am 35 years old, about 5'7", overweight at 165 lbs., with an average-size dick. I didn't get a taste for cocksucking until I was 27. At that time I had lost a lot of weight, was thin and attractive, and I started going to bars. I quickly became a regular at the International Stud (now defunct) on Greenwich Street in Greenwich Village. The Stud became like a second home to me and I went 4–5 times a week, coming in from Brooklyn where I lived.

When I first started going I would spend most of the evening in the front room playing pool and pinball. I would occasionally sneak into the back, sit on a bench in the thick of the action, and just watch. I was afraid to get involved, partly because I didn't think I could satisfy anyone. Also, the whole idea of just putting my hand out and touching the private parts of a stranger was new to me. Once I got used to the idea, for a long time I confined my activities to feeling the asses and cocks of guys who were having sex with others.

I used poppers a lot and it happened that my popper habit started at the same time I got into cocksucking. I remember the first time: one the regulars of the bar was a large, stocky (but not fat) young guy with a cute face and straight blond hair. His dick was obviously large and always hung several inches down his leg. I had wanted him for a long time. One night I found myself standing near him in the back (which was always crowded so that guys got pushed up against each other). I reached out and started groping him. He was receptive so I took his cock out.

At that moment someone handed him some poppers which he handed to me. The poppers sent such a shot of anticipation through me that I felt faint. His cock was long, thick, and straight, and I sucked it for a long time. The poppers made the experience unbelievably vivid. Finally, he came without making a sound. After that I was hooked on poppers and cocksucking.

The best man I ever sucked was a Puerto Rican named Alberto who also frequented the Stud. Alberto was 41 years old and looked much younger. The first time I saw him he was leaning against the back wall of the backroom. He was about 6'2" tall, lean, and had a real seductive look to him.

I started to grope him and he was receptive. His cock felt substantial, and when I opened his jeans I had to use both hands to pull it all out. His cock was cut, about 8" and thick, and nearly straight with perhaps a slight curve downward. The best part, though, was his balls: they were unusually large, round, and plump. The balls inside the sack were large and the sack itself was large, round, and firm. I was never able to get even one of his balls into my mouth, much less both.

In the months to come I sucked Alberto perhaps 8–10 times. He really knew how to get sucked. He would lean against the wall with his hips thrust forward. I would get on my kees and suck him slowly, using my hands and mouth together, and massaging his balls at the same time. He would slowly grind his hips as I sucked. When I would lick his balls, he would grind them into my face. I would alternate sucking his cock and balls and rubbing my face into his genitals.

Sucking Alberto was great because there was always a feeling of fullness: my hands were full, my mouth was full. I didn't have to scale down my hunger to fit smaller equipment.

Brandt Gets His Butt-Hole Licked.

When he would be done, everything would be wet. He would leave his cock out and let me play with it afterwards. He loved being touched and I could grope him for hours. I still have vivid fantasies about him and wish I could see him again.

Alberto was a bit of a degenerate. According to him, he went through an altruistic period when he was younger but then became cynical and bitter. He told me that he drank two quarts of beer every night. He had a boyfriend about his age who was emotionally dependent on him and when Alberto would start to feel cooped up he would go to a backroom and fool around. In the time that I knew him he occasionally talked about leaving his lover for me but of course that never happened.

Cocksucking wasn't the only thing I did at the Stud. I also picked up several one-night stands. One of them was named Brandt. Brandt

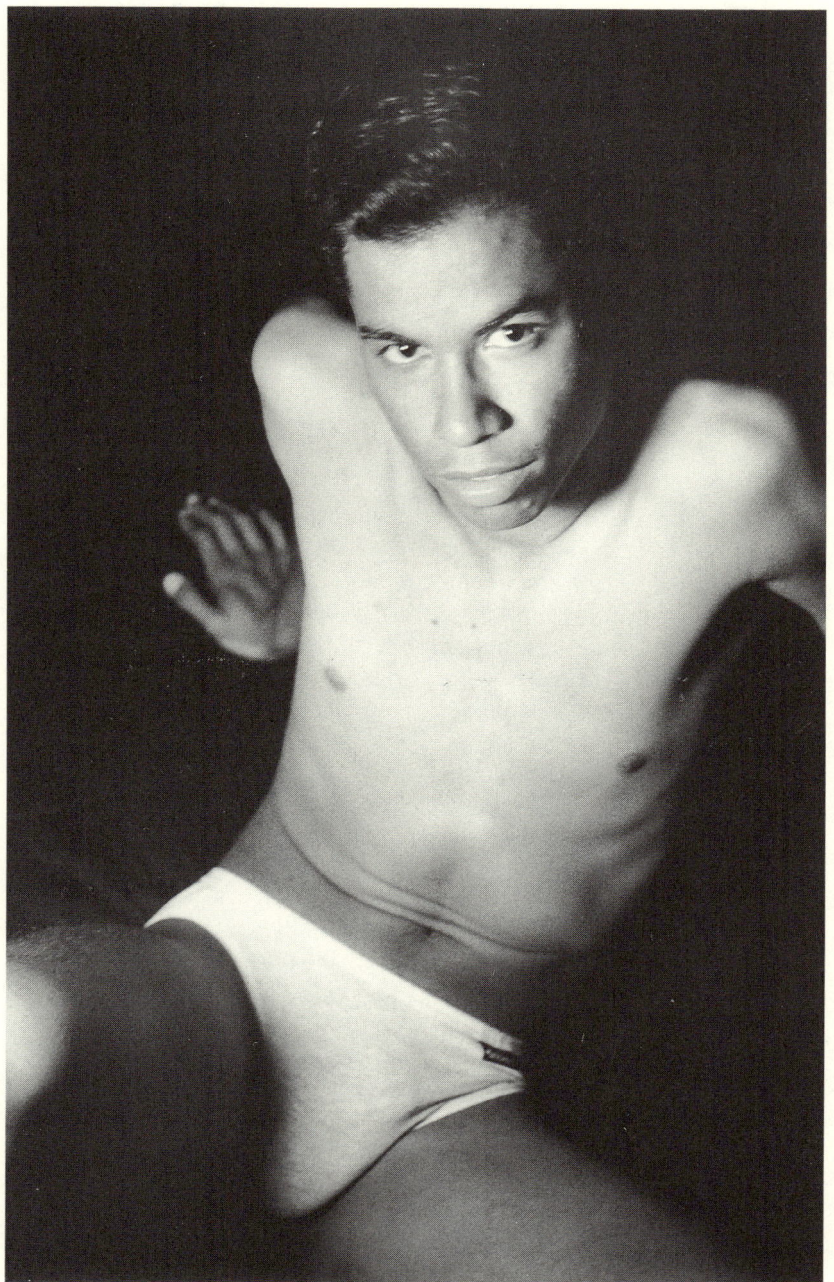

was 29 and very handsome, with classic facial features and hair that always sat just right. He had one of those athletic-type bodies that are hard all over, even when the muscles are relaxed, and he had a slender waist and hips. His hardness may have been genetic since, according to him, he was not athletic. He did do regular calisthenics, though, and his chest was very well developed—his pecs were large and round and I couldn't keep my hands off them. His cock was a bit less than average—about 5" and average width—but I didn't mind. He was such a turn on it didn't matter.

We met in the backroom when it was not crowded. We kissed for awhile and then went to his place. Our bodies fit together like they were made for each other. He fucked me twice and I fucked him once, and I rimmed him. We kissed passionately throughout. I know that I was satisfying him from the way he reacted but I was tense the whole time because I just couldn't believe that I was in bed with such a gorgeous guy. I was pretty insecure in those days and I was not as unattractive as I believed.

Of all the one-night stands I've had, Brandt is the one that I would have liked to see again, but I really screwed it up in a royal fashion. First, I came down with amoebic dysentery; and since I had rimmed him I implied on the phone that he may have given it to me. Also, I called him too many times, each time getting angrier that he was not calling me back. If I had been more relaxed about the whole thing I am sure he would have called me at some point, but my attitude scared him off.

Finally I saw him at the Stud. I was so proud and resentful that I ignored him all night. He spent a long time watching me play pool and I know I could have had him if only I had changed my attitude. What a dope I was.

One of the most exciting experiences I ever had was when I was 23 or 24, before my Stud days. At that time I was also in a thin period and I had a lover who was five years younger. My lover had a friend named Warren who was about his age (18–19) and was a light-skinned black, very cute, and on the small side, about 5'6" and slim. My boyfriend had known him since adolescence. It seems that they had been fooling around for awhile: they would watch TV together or talk and then Warren would pretend to be tired and fall asleep, at which point my lover would go down on him. When my lover told me that Warren's cock was huge, I decided I wanted a piece of the action.

At that time my lover and I lived in adjoining furnished rooms with sliding doors between. He invited Warren over one night. Late at night we were talking in my room and Warren, who knew what was up, pretended that he was tired and started to fall asleep. My lover left the room and I started to grope Warren. He was wearing short-shorts and his cock made a long, thick bulge pointing straight up.

I unzipped his shorts and took them down. His cock was perhaps 9", cut, shapely, and very thick, easily twice the thickness of my own, with nice round balls.

At that time I hadn't yet learned the joys of cocksucking and at first I jerked him dry, then with lotion, and then I took my clothes and lay on top of him and ground my cock into his. All this time he made not one motion and pretended to be asleep.

Now some men might not like that kind of scene but I loved it. His pretending to be asleep meant that he couldn't tell me what to do. I could have done anything with him. (Too bad I didn't have more imagination.) He came after about 20 minutes of jerking and rubbing.

What made this experience so exciting was just the *type* that Warren was: small, slender, cute, boyish, sweet, with a huge dick. That combination has always made me wild.

There are two things about this experience that I am not proud of, however: first, my lover spent the entire time in his room upset and on the verge of tears. He had set the scene up for me and Warren because he knew I wanted it, but he didn't like it.

Second, Warren was a confused and lonely young man and I think the last thing he needed was to be sexually exploited. My hunger for cock was just so insatiable that I couldn't resist.

The biggest cock I ever had was at the Christopher Street Book Store when I was about 31. I was downstairs and I had my eye on a white fellow who looked about 27–28, 5'10", slender and lanky, with long hair, and dressed normally in black jeans. He had a slightly hippy-ish look to him, or a rock musician look. At one point he disappeared into a large, dark area and I followed. When I reached out my hand and felt him, a shot of adrenalin went through me. What I felt was at least a foot long, very thick, rock hard, and jutting straight down his left pant leg more than halfway to his knee.

His cock, it turned out, was not only huge but shapely—unlike a lot of huge cocks which are hose-like—and had a nice, gentle curve to the shaft and a large, shapely head. The skin of it was light-colored, even milky. (I don't recall what the balls were like.)

Unfortunately, the first electric grope turned out to be the best part of it. I could only get my mouth halfway down on it and I couldn't keep my teeth out of the way. Deep-throating, which I am not good at anyway, was impossible. In addition, his cock wouldn't stay hard; it fluctuated from hard to semi-hard almost continuously.

I wondered at the time how he could get a hard on without getting faint from lack of blood.

I still harbor residual feelings of guilt for having been promiscuous. Writing down my experiences somehow legitimizes them.

With the AIDS epidemic raging, I have had to curtail my activities. I stopped going to back rooms and parks (partly because of the epidemic and partly because I was roughed up by fag-bashers the last time I went to the park). Instead, I started placing ads in the *New York Native* for men who liked to be sucked. Several of the men who answered my ad were interesting but with the exception of one, I never saw any of them more than four times.

"I get 2 or 3 loads every time I see him."

My favorite was Tom. Tom was 29 and short, about 5'6", and boyishly cute. He had dark hair and a compact body with great arms. His cock was cut, 7" (which I consider ample), sensuously curved toward his belly, and slender without being thin. The mild slenderness of his cock made it seem very long, which was a turn on.

I only sucked Tom twice, but they were two wonderful sucks. Tom had a very hard cock which was always up. He had great control over his orgasms and could go indefinitely without shooting until he or I decided it was time, at which point he would come within a minute or so. This was great because I could suck as fast or slow, hard or soft as I liked without fearing that he would pop unexpectedly.

Both blow jobs lasted a long time. I would start out slow and gradually work us both in a heightened state. After about ten minutes of sucking, Tom would start to utter an involuntary, obvious ecstasy; his long hard cock, his tight little body, and his nice personality were out of this world.

Unfortunately, Tom had a reoccurence of amoebas and stopped seeing me because he didn't want to infect me. After that he moved away.

Another fellow who answered my ad who was great to suck was Walter. Walter was 38, Italian, medium height and build, and had a wonderful cock that was about 6-1/2" and thick. I saw him only four times but they were good. Walter would lie across his bed with his feet hanging over the side and I would crouch between his legs. He would lie motionless, sometimes moaning, and sometimes watching me and saying things like, "Suck that big dick" or "Do you like that big dick?" Usually I don't enjoy such talk but from him I liked it. His legs were muscular and thick and his stomach was firm, so from my vantage point between his legs he was a real turn on.

Walter lost interest, however—why, I'm not sure. I think that screwing was his main interest. In addition, within a 40-day period, as

I recall, his best friend and two others died of AIDS and he got paranoid. (He hadn't had a sexual relationship with any of them, which I was glad to hear.) Also, Walter was immature; he was the "love 'em and leave 'em" sort who doesn't like to be friends with his ex-partners. Afterwards, when I would encounter him in the subway, it was obviously a pain for him to say hello and be friendly for a short while and he would walk away if he thought I hadn't seen him.

Right now I'm seeing a fellow who answered my ad who's very likable. His name is Andre, he's 26, about 5'7", and very thin. I get two or three of his loads every time I see him (36 loads so far). His cock is average length and a bit wider than my average-width cock, but sometimes when I'm horny it can seem much bigger. Andre isn't quite as responsive as I'd like—he doesn't moan much and not much of a "rhythm" develops between us—but he's always hard and can come repeatedly. I think we're becoming friends but I'm not sure.

I have had a total of four ads in the *Native* and each time I get 10–20 responses. Of those, about half went into the basket for various reasons, two or three would be eliminated after talking on the phone, one or two I would see and not like, and one I would like.

A lot of guys misrepresented themselves—not purposely I think; it's just that they thought they were hotter than they were.

Security Analyst, 23, Gets Hard On in Office.

One young fellow who was not bad looking turned me off because he wore a wig and also because, when I started to suck, he reacted in a giddy, un-sexy way.

Another fellow who said he was handsome might have been so to another man but to me he looked prematurely middle-aged.

Another was just plain fat and dull.

I've had two guys in their forties with huge cocks who couldn't keep them hard. One of them had a pessimistic outlook on life that eventually turned me off.

Another fellow wasn't happy being sucked but had to fuck my mouth in a rushed, unrelenting way.

One other man, who was tall and broad, was very dull and had a very small cock that wouldn't stay hard.

Quite frankly, I do better in parks and back rooms, but they are too dangerous and disease-ridden.

I'd like to tell you about the sexiest experience I've ever had that didn't include sex: I am a word-processor operator and I worked frequently on the evening shift at one of the big investment bankers. One of the analysts was named Bob. Bob was 23 and had a very friendly and outgoing personality. He was also very handsome, with a magnificent body. He told me that he had been an athlete all through high school and college and that he had played at almost every sport at one time or another. Bob was Irish, about 5'10", with sandy brown hair.

He was a "hands on" kind of person; he would frequently slap my back, shake my hand, squeeze my arm, or put his hand on my shoulder, always with a warm smile on his face. Every time I was around him I got excited.

Finally I decided to let him know I was gay. One day while talking to him on the phone I mentioned my boyfriend, and after that our relationship changed. He stopped being so "hands on"—not because he was prejudiced or homophobic but because there was clearly a sexual element in our relationship. It was clear to me that Bob had fooled around with guys at some point but now considered himself "straight."

Bob was more tense now in my company and it was a sexual tension. For example, he would glance at my crotch on occasion, which he never did before. One day he stepped into my office to say hello and instantly started to raise a hard on in his pants, which I don't think he expected to happen. He made a hasty exit but I was able to delay him for a few moments. That was the only time I was certain he was getting hard; his cock always showed a little in his pants and he knew that I always noticed it.

The sexiest thing Bob ever did was on those evenings when we would work together late into the night and, as exhaustion set in, inhibitions would drop. He would walk into my office for one reason or another—usually to get a document I had just typed—and he would stand right next to me, at my side. I would then slowly swivel my chair so that my shoulder pressed into his groin. He wouldn't move—he just stood there several minutes examining his document with my shoulder in his crotch. I regret to this day that I didn't put my hand up and grab him. It would have shocked him, but it might have been just what he was waiting for. He might have let me blow him, which was all that I wanted.

Another co-worker that I would have loved to get was named Alex. He was a lawyer at my present firm and left here only about six months ago. He was in his late 20s, blond, and about 5'6" but appeared much taller because his shoulders were so broad.

Paint Clerk, 20, Doesn't Hide His Hard On.

Alex had been a gymnast in school and he still had that gymnast's body—muscular, well-defined chest, shoulders, and arms with a slim waist and hips. He caught my attention because of his habit of standing back from the urinal with his hands on his hips while pissing. He had a huge, circumcised cock that would hang straight down. More than once I followed him into the john so I could get a glimpse of it.He must have been a hot teenager.

In my neighborhood there is a paint store. One day about four years ago I went in to buy some paint. While my paint was being mixed, two young men walked in carrying some boards. They were both attractive but one of them, about 20, took my breath away. The only word to describe him was voluptuous. He was about 5'10", large, with a curvaceous muscular body, neatly cut brown hair, blue eyes, and a face so handsome it belonged in the movies. He still had that wonderful, unadulterated flush of youth that usually only teenagers have.

Much to my surprise, after the two put their boards away, the one I liked immediately came up to me to see if I needed help. As he packaged my paint, we made small talk and I noticed that he was giving me frequent, penetrating glances. It dawned on me that he was interested when I looked down at his crotch (for the tenth time) and saw that he had a hard on.

He made no attempt to hide it and I was surprised at how unabashed he was, considering that anyone could have seen it. It turned out that he knew how to refinish floors so we made an appointment for him to look at my floor the following day after he got out of school.

When he arrived the following day it was obvious that he wasn't really interested in the floor. On that pretext, however, I took him in to look at my bedroom floor. After a few moments I grabbed his crotch and we started kissing. That started a relationship that lasted only a couple months and wasn't very satisfying, but I'm still glad it happened.

His name was Kenneth and he was Irish. He liked to kiss and nothing else. At first that was just fine: I had been going through a period of anonymous sex and hadn't had any real affection for more than a year. He was a superb kisser, too: we would take off our clothes and he would lay that magnificent body on top of mine and kiss me in the most passionate way, while grinding his crotch into mine.

It was very tender. After awhile, however, the kissing wore thin and I wanted more. Also, he had a girlfriend that he took places while I was kept at home like a mistress. I felt helpless to get what I wanted out of the relationship and I became very critical. I finally broke it off when I realized that I was turning into a prick.

It gave me a kick that his straight-laced parents had no idea of what was going on. Everytime I walked into their store I wanted to laugh. A couple of years earlier Ken had confessed his homosexuality to them and they had sent him to a shrink to get cured. He went back into the closet and pretended to be "straight" (which explained his girlfriend). Little did his parents know that he was making it with every guy that he could.

I later ran into Ken at the bank. I had forgotten how handsome he really is. I had also forgotten how sweet he is. In fact it's his sweetness that makes him so handsome. I have to admit that I longed for him as we talked.

He told me that on one crazy day in which he and his girlfriend went into Manhattan to see the sights, he proposed to her. Days or weeks later (he didn't say how long) he came to his senses and called it off. He did this by writing letters to his girlfriend and parents telling them that he was gay—and then he disappeared for a week (I wouldn't have wanted to be there either). Not long after that he moved into his own apartment, which he now shares with a lover. Sometimes sanity wins out.

Chased, Pushed, and Kicked By Two Troubled Teens.

I've had some pretty good experiences in parks. Two summers ago I cruised Forest Park near my home in Kew Gardens. I stopped early the following summer when two boys jumped out of their car, chased me, and pushed me around and kicked my legs (happily, they were wearing sneakers). That was the first time I had had an experience that went beyond name-calling and it scared me off the park for good.

You should have seen the look of obsession on their faces. To them I wasn't a human being, just an object of hate. I feel sorry for them although I wouldn't mind if either of them met a sudden death (my generosity goes only so far).

I learned from this experience that danger is fun *before* you get hurt. Once you've been attacked danger loses it allure. It was a frightening and painful experience for me (even though I wasn't physically hurt); I would rather not recount the details at this time.

The park scene was bad in other ways: once I tripped over a wire that someone had stretched across a darkened path and there was a lunatic who periodically set off large firecrackers in the woods.

The teenagers were the worst of it, however. They would park on the road bordering the park and sometimes hoot at the gay men cruising. I heard stories of gangs hiding in the bushes and attacking gays;

there was at least one murder.

I would arrive at the park anywhere from 9 P.M. until midnight, which was when the heaviest traffic started. Going to the park was both exciting and nerve-wracking. It made me nervous—a definite inconvenience. Because of the danger it was never boring, even when I didn't score. I frequently left the park if I sensed danger.

All I liked to do was to suck. The thought of partially undressing in order to fuck or get sucked didn't appeal to me. If I saw a man I liked I would carefully approach him and give him a grope. If he was receptive I went down on him. I never got more than two or three men in one night.

I have little to give in the way of characterizations; in sucking cock in the park, you don't get to know anyone. One man whom I sucked several times was about 30, short dark hair, nicely proportioned body, with a dick that was about 7-1/2" and moderately thick. He had nice balls too, that I cupped with my hands while I sucked him. (I like balls that are big enough to "cup.") We had a good rapport. His name was Christopher and I sucked him a total of four or five time on two evenings.

One man who I remember well but sucked for only a short time was a short young man. He was squat but not fat and looked Irish, with wavy red hair. He was wearing short, tight, thin, gray gym shorts that showed a huge cock. That particular evening he walked up and down the sidewalks, back and forth, almost never pausing. I couldn't approach him because he never seemed to stop, so I gave up. Later I was sucking a large man with a large cock on the inner sidewalk when the short fellow walked up and took his cock out. His cock was bigger than the big man's cock and I started sucking him. Apparently he was interested in the big man because he left when the big man left a few moments later. He confirmed my belief that the biggest cocks are on small guys.

"He made me stop so he wouldn't come."

One blow job I remember was very late at night. He was a young, nice-looking man with liquor on his breath. I took him into the park to a secluded tree and sucked him. His cock was average length but thick. I remember him so well because he really enjoyed it; he made me stop several times so he wouldn't come too soon. Afterwards, he was very appreciative. I gave him my number but he never called.

I sucked one fellow who was average looking and very thin. At first I ignored him because he had a large brown mole on his face that was a turn-off; but somebody told me he had a big cock so I zeroed in on him. His cock was long and thick and his balls were small ("all that

71

meat and no potatoes"). He made not a sound while I blew him but he held his hips in just the right way and I could feel the energy building up in his groin before he exploded.

I met a fellow in Forest Park who liked to play dead. I had noticed him on several occasions but ignored him because his body looked a little soft and fat. It was late, however, and there were just a few of us left, so I decided what the hell.

When he saw I was interested he left a note on a rock and then walked about 20 yards into the park. The note said: "MY FANTASY IS I PLAY THE DEAD JOGGER, YOU FIND MY DEAD BODY. DO WHAT YOU WANT WITH IT. RAPE IT, SUCK IT, FUCK IT, ETC. THAN (sic) DUMP IT OVER AND GO AWAY. *NO TALKING PLEASE*. JUST QUICK ACTION IF INTERESTED."

I followed him about 200 yards into the park to a small clearing. He got there before me and when I arrived he was sprawled out "dead." I gave his foot a kick and said, "Gee, I wonder who this is,"or something to that effect (I figured that kind of talk was OK). I then pulled his clothes open and sucked him for a long time. I tried to fuck him, but there was no lubrication and he was tight.

He had a great cock. It was thick at the base with a moderate taper toward the head and curved towards his belly in just the way I like. His cock was uncut but the foreskin was short and disappeared when he got hard, leaving just a nice looseness to the skin.

I really got into the fantasy. I liked the feeling of being totally in control. I didn't have to worry about whether he was going to react positively or negatively or whether I was satisfying him. He must have been really dead, however, because 20 minutes of hard sucking didn't produce an orgasm.

I still have his note.

The best experience I ever had in a park was in Riverside Park about a year ago. I had noticed a handsome, dark-haired fellow several times and finally got up the nerve to approach him. I started to grope him and he took out a very nice, wide, thick cock that gently curved towards his belly. I started to go down on him but he stopped me, wanting a more secluded spot. We must have tried about four spots before we found one down near the river. He lay back on the grass and I made him come in no time—much too soon in fact.

I have found that different kinds of cocks are better in different positions. This fellow's equipment was most exciting when he was on his back; it seemed to be more prominent that way. My friend Alberto, whom I mentioned earlier, was best to suck when he was standing; I got him on a bed once and it was awkward. A couple men's cocks seemed to come to life only when they straddled my face, and other men have been good sitting on a chair or lying with their feet over the edge of a bed. Each man is best savored in his own best position.

The last blow job that I gave my current suckee, Andre, was possibly the best (we're now up to 41). I previously said that the chemistry between us was not entirely good, mainly because he comes very quickly and, consequently, there was never any build-up before his orgasm. This last time, however, I sucked him very gently and slowly, stopping frequently when he was on the verge of coming. I managed to prolong it and it turned out to be great for both of us. I realize now that a good cocksucker doesn't look for excuses but adjusts himself to the situation. Giving a blow job is like playing an instrument; a good musician can make any instrument sound good.

Street Youth Gets Hard On; It Bounces As He Walks.

There is a new mail boy at my firm. He is about 5'7" and very slender, with blond hair; very young and boyish, yet self confident. The first time I saw him I *knew* that he was well hung, having known his physical type before. Today he was "showing" for the first time; he was wearing his cock straight up under the zipper of his tight office pants. It looked nice and long. I have decided to try and get him, even though there is a risk of losing my job.

(In the event that The Reverend Jimmy Swaggart or any of his partners in crime is reading this, by "get" I do not mean that I'm going to kill him, as the word means in the "straight" vernacular; I merely mean that I am going to suck him or, in other words, exalt him.)

Today on the subway I sat across from a man with a large, round, lumpy bulge in his tight pants. This man had me pegged before my ass even hit the seat. He let his crotch show and glanced at me frequently. His genitals bulged out on both sides of his zipper and the bulge moved and shifted as he moved. At one point when he thought I wasn't looking, he gently caressed it with his fingers. I couldn't tell if he was looking for action or was just an exhibitionist. Unfortunately, I was on my way to work and didn't have time to find out.

A week ago as I was walking up Lefferts Boulevard in my neighborhood of Kew Gardens, a man crossed the street in front of me and continued down Metropolitan Avenue. He was a large, "strapping," dark-haired young man with an ample figure—i.e., a full musculature with just enough padding to make him extra sexy. He was wearing cowboy boots and *very* tight blue jeans that hugged his plump, round ass obscenely. Up front, his large cock pressed straight out to the left, perfectly outlined by the thick material. It looked to be at least five inches soft and very thick.

I followed him into a small food market but got to see little more, as he kept his back turned while he talked to a store clerk.

About a week before, I was walking on Lefferts Boulevard to one of the magazine stores when I was passed by a tall, thin teenager with a handsome face, whose very long, very hard, very erect cock jutted straight out to the left and slightly downward, bouncing as he walked. He must have been wearing boxer shorts or nothing under his light brown corduroys.

I especially love to look at a bulging crotch when it is obvious that the owner has taken care to put it on display. The best of these I saw about a year ago on the subway. When I got my first glimps of this fellow my eyes nearly popped. He was young (mid 20s), with olive skin and dark hair, and an attractive, well-proportioned body. It was summer and he was wearing very tight, *very* thin, summer-weight gray pants with no underwear. The thin cloth positively clung to his ample genitals, which hung to one side, outlining them perfectly. His pants weren't so tight that there wasn't any "play," and when he moved his genitals jiggled and bounced. He occasionally looked down at them and appeared to be uncomfortably self conscious, as if this kind of exhibitionism were new to him. We left the train at the same stop and I made sure I was behind him on the escalator. Happily, he leaned against the railing in such a way that I was able to get a few more glimpses.

Stonewall Cowboy Gets Fucked in Mouth.

There's a fellow in my neighborhood who sports a similarly well-defined crotch. He's a big young man, at least 6'3", stocky, and well muscled. The times I've seen him he's been wearing super-tight pants—usually white jeans—that ride up into the crack of his crotch so that his large cock and balls hang to one side, perfectly outlined from base to tip. (No underpants, naturally.) Once he had a semi-hard on and it was a big one. That semi-hard on was one of the hottest things I have ever seen.

Once years ago when I was riding the subway, I was walking from car to car when the sight of a nice round bulge caused me to stop dead in my tracks. It was attached to a large, handsome, Italian-looking young man. He was wearing black corduroys. I sat down across from him and he gave me a curious look, apparently because of the way I had stopped so suddenly.

Then, along came another faggot who also stopped short and took a position next to mine, leaning against a door. The man looked at the other faggot and then at me, at which point he must have realized what was happening because he looked down at his crotch. He made no motion to cover himself. Instead, he delicately removed two pieces of lint from his muscular thigh and got out at the next stop.

Once when I was applying for a job at an employment agency I saw a truly remarkable crotch. The agent gave me an application and asked me to fill it out. He was a young, thin, attractive black fellow whom I had met once before. While I filled out the form, he talked on the phone—apparently a personal call. I brought him the application and then asked for the key to the men's room. He had to stand up to get it and I gaped at what I saw. He had a long, thick hard on going down his leg. It looked to be nine or ten inches. Apparently the person he had been talking to had gotten him hot.

We walked into another room so he could get the key from another man—who, by the way, covetously and enviously glared at the agent's erection. The agent knew that his member was showing and made no attempt to hide it.

I hoped he would follow me into the men's room, but he didn't.

Years later I met this fellow again at a company where we were both working. he was cold to me, didn't show anything, and stank. So much for him.

The most magnificent crotch I ever saw was less than a year ago. I was walking along 23rd Street to my friend Ruth's apartment. (She asked for a mention.) I passed a man who looked gay. He was about six feet, had medium-light short hair, and a slender build. In the style of the day he was wearing tight sweat pants and a T-shirt. Hanging down one leg more than halfway down his knee was a cigar-shaped cock that looked to be ten inches or more and *very* thick. The sweat pants were loose enough so that his cock flopped with each step but tight enough so that I could clearly see the glans of his magnificent instrument. He also ad a pair of large, round hanging balls that bounced nicely.

I immediately turned and followed. I stood next to him at a corner while he waited for a light; and even though he noticed me, I couldn't bring myself to blurt out that I wanted his cock in my mouth.

I might have followed him further but decided that I shouldn't keep Ruth waiting, as I had always given her ahard time when she was late for me.

I remember one experience at the International Stud. I had been playing pinball with some of the regulars when up walked a very handsome man in cowboy garb. He was the strong, silent type. He joined our pinball game and the rest of us talked among ourselves about how good looking he was and whether any of us might get him. Suddenly he turned to me, grabbed me, and gave me a long, passionate kiss, right in front of everybody. I was so incredulous that I burst out laughing in the middle of the kiss, which did not deter him. I ended up going home with him to New Jersey.

He enjoyed sucking me and allowed me to fuck his mouth as if it were his asshole.

He was about 30 and told me that he had been at the Stonewall when it was raided by the police. He said that he adopted the cowboy garb because it suited him. I believe that he felt that his masculinity was compromised by his homosexuality, and this was his way of compensating. »«

"I KISSED THAT PREPPY ASS."

I was out of work and it was May and I signed on as a waiter at a resort hotel in the mountains of upstate New York. The job was easy. I served breakfast, lunch and dinner with breaks in between and most nights off. I had room and board, use of facilities, fair weekly pay, and tips.

There were waiters and waitresses. The waiters were evenly divided: those who were looking to hump the female guests and those who were looking to be humped by the personalities in summer stock at the tent adjacent to the grounds where tired old musicals were being recycled.

It wasn't a bad deal, but after a few days of swimming and sunning I found myself in need of a little physical excitement. The one male who seemed capable of giving this excitement was the golf pro—tall, muscular, bronzed; you know. But rumor had it that he was kept busy plowing the older females between golf lessons.

There was a mill town several miles away and a jitney—courtesy of the hotel—which made periodic trips there so guests could do some shopping. One day between lunch and dinner I availed myself of the service and arrived in a matter of minutes into that town. After making a few purchases, I stopped in a bar redolent of young blue collars and ordered myself a beer. The lads had finished work, had gotten themselves into clean sport shirts and pants, and I had a couple of beers at the sight of them. They played the machines, they played the juke box, and I gulped down a few more beers than I'd intended. Surrounded by all that muscle, I hesitated to be blatant and I left without anything happening.

It was ten thirty and the last jitney back to the hotel left at eleven. The stop was going toward the highway and right next door was a large ice cream store where you could get cones, dishes, milk shakes, whatever. The boys behind the counter were obviously preppy, ranging from early college back to late high school. They wore white pants spotted with melted ice cream and looked as sexy that way as any of the factory workers at the bar.

I continued doing that bar when I came into town with no luck, and found myself stopping earlier and earlier in the ice cream store. They really were sexy boys and being without sex since I took my job, I appreciated the hell out of them.

On afternoon, free from having to serve dinner, I took the jitney and spent a lot of time in the millhand bar, getting tipsy, and finally making out with a young blue collar who escorted me to a neighboring park and allowed me to suck him off. It was a perfunctory blow job and after it was over he zipped up and left me. It was my first in a month but not enough fun to make up for the fact that I had missed the jitney and could either hitch hike or walk to the hotel.

I went back to the pick up spot next to the ice cream parking lot and stood a few minutes before undertaking the long journey. Along came Tommy, just closing the store. He crossed the parking lot, got into his jalopy, and pulled up alongside me. I told him I'd missed my bus and he said, "Get in; I'll take you back."

Now over the past weeks I'd flirted outrageously with these lads. One night when one of them asked if I'd ever jerked sodas I had said, "No, but I can make a banana SPIT," and they all got a kick out of it and passed it on, and we kidded along these lines every time I went in the place.

Now, sitting alongside Tommy, who was tall and blond in his freshman year in college, I was aware once again that young men his age, preppy or blue collar, like to cum a lot, and although I didn't exactly nudge against him my leg wasn't too far away from his.

As we rode, he said, "Do you have a girl back in the city?" and I said "no." He said, "The guys were wondering."

I cleared up the matter at once. "I like boys."

He said, "We weren't sure if it was an act."

Then, after a mile or so, "So you can make a banana spit?"

"Depends on how ripe it is," I said, and he took my hand and placed it over his young dick, saying, "It's ripe," and it sure was. Up ahead was a roadside rest area deserted at this hour and as I continued to press my fingers he eased into it and parked under a clump of trees.

After the hurry-up job on the mill boy I was in no mood to repeat that performance and I began to get rid of those work-stained white pants; my hands working his thighs and his teenage ass before I lowered my head, soon sucking over the entire area of his hot crotch.

I licked those preppy balls, kissed that preppy ass, and gave him a blow job the mill hand could have had if he were not in such a goddam hurry.

77

Takes 6 in Ass Whilst Sucking 6 Off.

When it was over, he sighed and, ever the preppy, said, "That was neat."

"You ever have it before?" I asked. He said yes. There was this queer kid back at school, but "never as good as this."

When we got to the hotel he asked me if I'd mind if he "told the guys." I said no, but "just don't get me run out of town."

"Don't worry," said he, "they're cool."

And they were. Cool but warm. When next I went into the store the atmosphere was friendly as ever but the banter became more pointed. Mike, a college sophomore, responded to my order of a cone by saying, "I hear you like it warm." And that same night he drove me back to the hotel in the same jalopy I'd ridden with Tommy and in the same rest area, served it up just that way.

Another night Dave, in his last year of high school, referred to the old joke: "How do you make a banana spit?"

"Easy if it's ripe," I answered.

He said, "Wanna find out?"

And he became number 3 in what was to be a wonderful summer. I did him in the same rest area, and so on. There were about 12 youths in various shifts and during the remaining weeks I worked my way through the entire crew. So busy was I that I stopped going to the bar to be frustrated by the factory boys.

All of these boys had names but soon they were all dick to me. The common experience seemed to unite them and they became buddies even if they weren't before. As for me, I was having a blast, especially with Tommy and Mike, who had the hottest blood of a hot-blooded crew.

My free time was given over entirely to these young men and hardly a night went by without my enjoying one or the other. Most of them used the same jalopy and it got so I hardly ever took the jitney back to the hotel and that rest area on the way became my personal background.

Back at the hotel, the staff—the strates and the others—assumed that since I kept so much to myself, I was neither one nor the other.

Summer was coming to an end and the kids were finishing up their jobs and getting ready to go back to school. One night about a week before Labor Day Tommy mentioned that his folks had a summer camp on the other side of the mill town and had given him permission to use it for an end of summer party for the guys. He asked me if I'd go, saying there would be lots of beer, hot dogs, and all that. I quickly agreed to attend.

I took the jitney to town that night and Tommy, who was off, drove me to the camp. By about 12 o'clock all 12 of the lads had assembled. It was a beery boys' night where we all got nicely smashed but not overpoweringly so. About two o'clock in the morning somebody suggested a swim and soon we were all skinny-dipping in the lake. We came back to the main room of the elaborate "camp" to dry before the large stone fireplace. We were all naked and full of good will and tipsy. I'd had sex with all of these boys and felt comfortable with them, so when somebody asked me if I ever took it in the ass I said, "a couple of times," and then, "back in the city a couple of times a night."

This got a big laugh and when someone suggested a gang bang it seemed perfectly natural, although I'd never done anything with these boys except blow them. I'd had a few threesomes in my time but had never been gang banged and the idea appealed to me. The idea appealed to all of us and I soon found myself crouched over in the center of the room with my hands on my ankles while the boys formed two lines on either end. A kid named Jack jumped me first and I began to suck off Jerry, who was first in the other line. I took them in relays, at ast 12 inches at a time, six in one hole and six in the other, and at the end of the first relay, nicely oiled in both holes, was having a great time.

So were the boys and so successful was the experiment that when the lads wanted to switch lines I was perfectly willing and we started all over again. Finally, bushed, we got into our clothes and, true to his word, Tommy drove me back to the hotel, where I only had time to shower and change before breakfast.

I got through that meal somehow; it only hurt when I walked.

It was fun but I would not recommend the activity for a novice. For resiliency my pussy is probably second to none, but consider it: ascribing to the 12 young men a minimum of six inches, my total intake was at the very least 36 inches (mouth) plus 36 inches (butt hole) for a total of 72 inches for the night. Surely a record.

After breakfast I visited the medicine chest in the community room. We had waitresses and there was some Tampax and also a jar of Vaseline. I had time before lunch for a hot bath/douche and liberally larded my box with grease, holding it in with Tampax, and was able to serve lunch with ease.

By dinner I was my chipper self. Still, because summer was over and I never saw any of the young men again, I felt their presence for quite some time. »«

BEACH HAS BAREASS BOYS, OLDER MEN IN TEENS, 20s.

It was the summer of 1943 on the south shore of L.I. in an area that emulated the so-called wealthy north shore. The German Bund marches had been halted on Sunrise Highway but the restricted golf clubs—"German only" and "German & German Jewish only"— were still in full regalia, as were the private beach clubs lining Atlantic Beach with their restrictions.

I was at my family's club when my friends walked down the beach from their family clubs to join me. Morty and Bobby belonged to lesser clubs and preferred to come over to my club, as it was the most prestigious. I was 11, Morty was 10, and Bobby was 9.

Morty suggested we sneak out through the back of one of the clubs that none of us belonged to and get on our bicycles and ride through Long Beach past Lido and go swimming at Point Lookout Beach, where we could swim nude. It was a wild, natural, undeveloped beach and everyone went bareassed.

Our mothers never knew we left the beach and thought we were taking a walk along the shore. The trip didn't take very long. Once we were there, we turned off the road onto a packed trail between the high reeds and series of high sand dunes.

I was raring to take off my bathing suit and run into the ocean but Morty said no and that we should all take a walk in different directions on the narrow walks through the reeds. I asked why and he said just do it and you'll find out. I was annoyed but walked away, down one of the paths between two sand dunes.

In a short while I came across a small open area where two older men (in their teens) were standing nude fondling each other. I didn't know what they were doing and just stood there watching out of curiosity. They saw me, smiled, and continued their games. I thought to myself I'd like someone to play with me like that.

I continued walking. The path got narrow again and started twisting. At one of the bends stood a much older man by himself. I started to squeeze by and he gently stopped me, put his hand on my shoulder, looked me in the eye, smiled, and started touching me all over. He took my hand and put in on the crotch of his bathing suit. It was the first time I ever felt another man's penis. It was very exciting. I felt myself get hard.

He slowly slid my bathing suit down and again took my hand and made motion to pull his down. Instead I put my hand inside his bathing suit and felt him, his large balls and hair. Then I pulled his suit down.

He took his bathing suit and put his arm through one of the leg holes. He then kissed me and I asked how old he was. He said 21. Boy was he old, I thought. He then ran off toward the ocean, his suit on his shoulder.

I continued walking, now nude, and came across a few groups, stood and watched once again, was groped a few times, and started to get bored. I walked to the ocean and met my two friends. They asked me how I liked it. I just laughed and so did they. They told me it was their second summer coming over to Point Lookout Beach.

We bicycled back to Atlantic Beach, sneaked through one of the clubs, and went back to our own clubs. The day was over.

Point Lookout beach became our gang of three's beach for the next 4 years. It was the Fire Island of the war years.

We continued our routine every few days all that summer. I started to notice young men hitchhiking from the point that the L.I. railroad station was in Long Beach. They all seemed to be good looking and neatly dressed in summer clothes, most carrying a little bag. I then saw them in the dunes undressing and either putting on a bathing suit, jock strap, or just walking around nude.

As I did this he went down on his knees and started to suck me. I came almost immediately. I watched him jerk himself off. I had never seen a man do this before. He shot his load almost 5 feet.

"I liked the smell of a man."

I turned 12 late in the summer; Bobby, 10, and Morty, 11. We always went our separate ways in the dunes. Morty was dark and effeminate, Bobby was an extreme beauty with thick curly white blond hair, and I was a curly redhead and had a scrubbed cute clean look. We look great together; we covered every look.

I learned to suck my first cock. I liked the smell of a man. One afternoon I had my first threesome with two freshmen college students, one of them uncut. I never saw an uncut 'til then.

It was late summer. Our parents all were away on vacation. We decided to see Fire Island and took Bobby's family's boat that was docked near home in the waterway leading to Great South Bay. We took it to what is now Cherry Grove; that was the Coast Guard station.

The Coast Guard sailors were amazed to see us arrive and helped us dock. Then they escorted us to the "shack," where you could get beer. They proceeded to feed us beers. Being so young we got drunk very fast. We then all went walking. One sailor had his arm around me. We each paired off and went our separate ways. The Coast Guard men were available.

Mine told me he was 17 years old and horny as hell and I looked like his redheaded girlfriend; did I ever fool around with a guy? I lied and said no but I would like to with him. He wanted to screw me but after seeing he was about 8 inches I said no way. I sucked him off. While I was doing it he displayed the most magnificent stomach muscles. He then to my amazement went down on me. When it was over he said that's the first time he ever sucked cock and he did it because I was so cute, young, and clean. At that point I only had a little reddish blond pubic fuzz though I was already hung over 6 inches. We made two other trips to F.I. that summer.

The summer of '43 passed. Morty, Bobby, and I wondered what happens in the dunes in the winter. We had learned the affectionate name of the dunes was "the Doings."

1944 passed as a duplicate of 1943. The Doings, Atlantic Beach, golf club, F.I. sailors.

1945: summer arrived; we continued our routine but one afternoon we met a group of teenagers from L.I. They had no idea we were so young. They took us to our first gay bar in W. Hempstead. It was exciting to find out we weren't alone on L.I., that there were lots of us. We made new friends that we were to have sex with in the winter.

One afternoon the boy across the street from my family's home asked me if I needed a ride to the beach. He was two years older than I and we didn't have much in common at that point. I had just reached 14; he was 16 and drove a car.

We got to the beach early and he said why don't we get undressed in his cabana. Peter was the best looking boy in the town. He had jet blue black curly hair, a magnificent full chest, defined stomach muscles, and smooth olive skin.

We were fully nude, about to put on our suits, when he looked down at my crotch and said, "Wow, you have red hair down there. I never saw that." Peter was considered the most macho man in high school; he was on all the teams. He said, "Can I touch it." I laughed and said sure. He started to get hard and became embarrassed. I grabbed his cock and got hard myself. He started to jerk me off and I did the same to him. We both came, put on our suits, and ran out to the pool and jumped in. I went home with him at the end of the day. I asked my parents if I could sleep over at his house that night because we wanted to go to the beach early and he had a car. They said it was O.K.

Gets First Rim Job.

We slept in the same bed. I waited for Peter to make the first move. He finally whispered, do I think we could do the same thing as we did that morning. I said yes but a little different this time. He said how? I said to lie back and relax. I went down on him. He let out a gasp and then a little moan.

He said he couldn't reciprocate but he'd jerk me off. Afterward he put his arms around me and we went to sleep.

Peter made me promise I would not tell anyone of what we were doing, not even my friends. I promised and we continued having sex and making love daily for over the next 4 years.

Years later Peter told me I was the only male he had ever had sex with. I believe him. He is now married with 4 children, fat, and bald.

I'll always think of those days and nights with Peter, Mr. Macho Man. Eventualy he sucked me and even allowed me fuck him. Our first fucks. I'll always remember the scar on his left butt.

Late summer, 1945, evening. I'm walking my dog. A good looking man of about 35 was standing on his front lawn a few blocks from home. He says it's real hot, heh? How about a cold drink, you look kind of warm. I said O.K. and went inside with him.

He put his arm around my shoulder. We sat on his patio in the garden in back of his home. He tells me his wife and family are away for the summer and he's a grass widow.

I look down at his crotch. Man, it is full. He catches me looking. He says he's kind of lonely, alone in his big house. My eyes are still on his crotch. He says when he was my age he was always curious what a grown man's cock was like. Do I want to see his? I said yes, but I was slightly embarrassed.

We went inside. He slid his pants down. He was wearing boxer shorts. He took my hands and made me unbutton his shirt. He had beautiful adult masculine hairy pecs. I put my hand through the slit in his shorts. it was fat, soft, and cut. He pulled his shorts down. It gradually got hard as I handled it and reached over 10 inches.

He said, "Well, what do you think?" I said it's the most beautiful cock I've ever seen and I hope one day to be as perfect as him.

He smiled, hugged me, and said, why don't I strip. I said I have to go home, though it wasn't true. I was a little afraid as I'd never been in a sex scene with an adult man.

He helped me out of my shirt and I chickened and said no. He offered me $50.00 and kissed me. I really wanted him. I took my clothes off. We lay down on a bed and he proceeded to tongue me all over, settling on my asshole, rimming me. It was the first time for that experience.

I came without my cock being touched, didn't lose my hard on, and to my surprise he got on his knees on the bed, arched his back, buried his face in the pillow, and asked me fuck him. I did, and came.

He put his arms around me and kissed me goodbye and said he hopes I'll visit him soon again.

When I went to bed that night and emptied my pockets I found the $50.00. I saw him several more times before his wife returned. Each time I found the $50.00.

I would have had sex without the money, he was so super, but I never gave the money back.

1946 came. It was my year of fully coming out, N.Y.C. bars, Point Lookout, learning to drive a car, meeting upper class gay society, Peter, leather bars, Village bars etc. The names have all been changed of the people but this is all true.

Dock Worker Strips in Park To Get Butt Whipped.

The war was over. I was going on 15 years, Morty was 14, and Bobby now 15. We were frequenting the bar in W. Hempstead, particularly on Sun. evenings when the first "gays" were really starting to settle the Grove (Cherry Grove) on F.I. and were returning to the city after the weekend.

Since building supplies were scarce and the large Long Island estates were being broken up to make room for the ticky-tacky houses to be built for the returning soldiers, the old gardeners' cottages from the estates became available and were grabbed up to be moved to the Grove. First by land and then by barge across Great South Bay and finally rolled on logs to their final site on stilts, to be named Tara, Shirley's Temple, Thimk Pimk, etc., and ditzed up. Belvedere came later.

The Coast Guard station was still there and so were the sailors. Point Lookout Beach became more exciting as now there were lots of "older" men that were now out of the services.

We were still sneaking out of our clubs in Atlantic Beach to spend the day at the Doings (Dunes) of P. Lookout. One late afternoon I had a long sex scene with a guy wearing jack boots and a black leather vest. This was strange to me because the beach was mostly preppie and N.Y.C. showbiz guys. He asked the three of us if we would like to take a ride to the city. Our parents once again were away so we said yes. He seemed kind of tough but at the same time educated and intelligent. He was 29, good looking, and very well built.

He had a car and we drove to N.Y. He asked us, do we ever go to any bars in N.Y.? We said no, it was our first time, which was true. He put the car in a garage near 42nd streeet and 6th Ave. and took us to a rough bar on 6th Ave. and 43rd St. where there were a lot of guys wearing leather, dungarees ("jeans" was not used at that time, came later), and western gear. We were frightened as we were used to seeing preppie and trendie clothing at the Long Island bars. It was frightening but that made it all the more exciting.

I was picked up by a blue collar muscled dock worker. We walked across 6th Ave. to Bryant Park behind the library on 42nd St., and went behind the statue. There were a multitude of men there having sex and in all kinds of dress from suits to dungarees. It was funny to see a guy with a suit jacket and tie, with no pants on, nude from the waist down, being fucked and sucked at the same time.

My new friend asked me to take my belt off. I did. He then stripped and told me to hit him as hard as I could across his ass with the buckle side and keep doing it and gradually work up his back.

First I couldn't do it, then I started to hit him harder and harder. all the guys around me stopped what they were doing and watched. He got a roaring 8-1/2–9 inch hard on. He finally told me to stop, bent over with his hands on the statue, and told me to fuck him. I did. His butt was so hard that it didn't even move as I pounded him. Guys were now kneeling with their faces at my friend's asshole watching. I had an explosive orgasm.

One guy standing next tome said, "Let me try that." He started to pump with such force my friend nearly lost his grip on the sttue. After, three others pounded him in succession.

At that point I left, went back to the bar, and picked up my friends. We took the L.I.R.R. back home to L.I. exhausted.

The next morning Peter woke me up. We went to Atlantic Beach and made love in his family's cabana. We spent the day and the night together and had sex several times.

100 Farmers, War Vets, Students Attend Orgy.

Every small town had to have their town "sissy" and we were no exception. His name was Andy and he came from one of the wealthiest families in town. He was a "pretty-boy" and had the first plastic surgery on his nose that any man in the area had. He was three years older than I and wanted to be a movie star. His father went so far as to buy him a bit part in a Betty Grable-Dan Dailey movie.

One afternoon Andy asked the three of us if we would like to go into the city that night. Our families belonged to the same beach club and I would see him there all the time. We went with him and he took us to the oldest Village bar at that time, called "Mary's," on 8th St. near 6th Ave.

We were introduced to several middle aged men who we were to learn came from old line American wealth and were socially prominent.

I was invited to several parties in the city and Southampton, L.I. The mixture in the bar was extraordinary, from men just out of the service going to college, starving artists, would-be actors, and two young men that were destined to become movie stars, one of the highest order.

I left the bar with a socialite and was driven in his limousine to a magnificent duplex apt. on 5th Ave. that had a double winding staircase in the entrance foyer and overlooked Central Park. I asked my new found friend how old he was and he said he was 40. He never asked my age.

We went to his bedroom and undressed. He had a circular bed. He had a body that was in great shape but soft; you could tell he had never done any physical work.

He tongue washed me all over for the second time in my life. I fucked him with him on his stomach then once with his legs over my shoulders. When I did that he came without being touched. He shot over my shoulder and it landed in the small of my back, trickling down the crack of my ass.

He drove me back downtown to pick up my friends and drove all of us back to L.I. Andy had disappeared. I slept with Peter that night even though it was late when I got there. There was no problem, as his family was away and he was home alone.

I learned how to drive that summer but I was still too young to have a license.

Morty's mother died. He was an only child and his father travelled for business, so he was by himself a lot. His father sold their house and took an apt. in the village and hired a maid to come in and take care of things during the day. The people in the apt. building kept their cars in the basement, which they only used on weekends, and Morty knew where the keys were kept by the attendant.

The town was changing. There were no more restrictions and a new group of people were moving in, namely the 7th Ave. garment manufacturers, though showbiz people were still excluded. A well known show person tried to buy a home at that time and found he couldn't. He became the most prominent television figure of the 1950s–60s.

School had started. It was now Oct. 1946. Morty called me to say he had a neighbor's car and would I like to drive us to W. Hempstead. I said yes. In W. Hempstead we found that a new bar had opened. It was an old grist mill with a barn behind it at the edge of Hempstead Lake

Park. We went there and found the barn was one large orgy. There were old time potato farmers, newly married returned soldiers living in the new tacky housing with their families, teenagers, as we were, and college students. It was like the porno videos that now try to imitate, only it was real. There sometimes were 100 or more men actively engaging in sex at one time in the barn.

At this point in my life I discovered I could have multiple orgasms without losing my hard on. I fucked, sucked, finger-fucked for the first time, bit, slapped, grabbed, groped, touched, felt, squeezed, hugged, kissed, pinched, pulled, rubbed, jerked off, and on & on. In later years I found that Morty had stolen the car.

Has Room at the St. Mortiz and an 11" Prick.

We took the L.I.R.R. into the city on weekends, went to Mary's, found the bar at the Bon Soir, and another, now a jazz club on 7th Ave. in the Village. We discovered there were several leather bars on 6th Ave. between 43–48 St. At one of the leather bars I met a nicely dressed man of 28. He looked out of place in a suit. He told me he was in the city from the mid-west on business. He was very handsome and well spoken. We left and went to his hotel.

He told me he was being trained for a job in Brazil. He was staying at the St. Moritz on 59th St. and the Park.

We undressed. He was wearing boxer shorts. I put my hand inside them and was overwhelmed. I had never felt such a large cock before. It became hard almost immediately, and must have been 11 inches long. His balls were small in comparison. His cock was cut. His back was covered in hair which felt good to touch.

He made tender love. I screwed him twice and he sucked me off once. He wanted to fuck me but I wouldn't let him. Instead he dry fucked me in my ass crack. A half hour after he came I sucked him off again.

He offered to keep me if I would go to Brazil with him. I said sure, not meaning it. He said he would send me the plane tickets which I didn't believe. Two weeks later tickets arrived with a visa for me to fill out. I sent the tickets back with no note and never heard from him again.

As the winter went on we went to N.Y. more often. I got very heavy into the S & M scene of the time. I loved working on someone's tits, C & B torture, bondage, etc. I was taught by some very patient masters.

I was still going home to Peter, who had no idea of what I was doing.

Andy had a younger brother who was very butch and a grade below me who was to enter the leather scene in the city, two years later, accidentally kill someone, and commit suicide in jail, which turned me off from the leather scene for 20 years.

My older brother returned from the Navy looking like he was in the wrong uniform, as he was very Germanic looking, 6'4" with extremely broad shoulders, narrow waist, naturally streaked straight blond hair, piercing blue eyes, very muscular especially his legs, square chinned with a deep cleft, and enormous hands. He looked like Hitler Youth.

He was hung as well as he looked. He had been away all the time I was entering my teens because of the war. Now he was only home for a short time as he was going away to college in N.C. and would only be home for holidays for the next 3 years as he was going to school 12 mos. a year to make up the lost war years.

We were never to become friends because of the war. We still are not close or even friends. I was hoping he might be a "bi" but I could not even have talks with him. He had become a beer and cigar man. He left soon after coming home.

1947 arrived. I still was having sex with Peter nearly every day and still going to the city with Morty and Bobby.

Spring came and we started to go to P. Lookout but the talk at the L.I. bars was that F.I. (Fire Island) was fast becoming the place. There now was a community in the Grove and a few houses were actually being built there.

Joe's ferry service to the Grove started. I started legally driving a car. My family still belonged to the beach club but now I didn't have to sneak away, I just said I'm going for a drive with my friends and took off. We started picking up hitchhikers in Long Beach and drove the car into the dunes in P. Lookout to fuck.

We drove out to the ferry in Sayville, spent the day in the Grove, and drove home in the evening. I couldn't legally drive in N.Y. City limits but we did anyway.

"We picked up many sailors."

My parents thought I was coming of age and I should be introduced to polite society. I reluctantly went with them to some Southampton L.I. Society parties. I was pleasantly surprised to see the middle age men I had met at Mary's in the Village at those parties. I enjoyed seeing their shock and embarrassment at seeing me at their parties.

We became more friendly and I was invited to spend a week and weekend at their summer homes. My parents were delighted that I was so easily accepted and gave their approval.

During one of these week's stays in Southampton at a prominent banking socialite's home he decided he would have a party and invited all of his gay friends. He hired a band and caterers. There were approximately 100 invited guests, some who brought friends with them.

The swimming pool was lit up, electric lights strung in lanterns, and a large striped canopy was put up covering a buffet. The party was very proper but with all the innuendos of being gay. I danced with a man for the first time. I was propositioned more times than I can remember. I finally settled on a very Ivy League man who was about 27–8. We went into the mansion and into one of the bedrooms. There were 5 men already carrying on in the room. We left and went into another bedroom that was also occupied by several men. We tried another three but they were all being used. Finally we opted for a large bedroom with two double beds, one occupied, the other free.

The two men in the room stopped and watched us get undressed. My new friend had a body that showed me he kept in shape at a gym, not muscular but no fat. He was hung only average.

We had started making love when he burst out crying, telling me all about his lover in the city and how he had carved his initials on his ass and then would invite his friends to do the same.

He turned over on his stomach and his ass was a mass of scars. He continued to talk and suddenly said, "Please carve your name on my ass and fuck me. There's a knife in my pocket." I said forget it. One of the other men in the room said, "I'll do it." He proceeded to cut my friend's butt. There was blood all over the sheets. He screwed him, got blood all over himself, and when he was finished his friend screwed him.

I was turned off by my friend but got very turned on by one of the other men in the room and ended up fucking him several times. He had a full head of pure white hair and jet black pubic hair and a beautiful hairless smooth body. I was shocked to find out later that he was in his 60s. He was rich.

We cleaned up the mess and rejoined the party.

Gay places in the city were opening one after another. Dior had come out with the "New Look" and interest in clothing became paramount, both men's & women's, after the boring look of the war years.

Eighth St. in the Village became the center for hip N.Y. gay life. Trendy, experimental, it was the Christopher st. of the late 40s and early 50s. Closet doors were opening. There were a few gay bar "raids" and closings.

Upper East Side bars were opening for the Ivy League with its elegant pretentions.

Bobby discovered a bar on W. 72nd St. near W.E. (West End) Ave., when he visited an aunt of his on W.E. Ave. It attracted showbiz types in a kind of raunchy setting. It was always good if we didn't make out in the Village.

We still continued going to P. Lookout Beach and discovered that the Lido Beach Hotel was now a discharge center for the Navy. It was right next to P. Lookout. It was an enormous 1920s Moorish resort hotel with a golf course, tennis courts, and swimming pool, and on the ocean. We picked up many sailors and went to the "Doings" with them to have sex.

Women for Public Relations, Men for Private Relations.

Summer ended and we began school but now I had a car. The local "straight" singles hangout was Anthony's in our town. As it was becoming more expedient to put up a "straight" front we started going there.

We soon found out so did a lot of other guys. We all made sure we were seen with girls and then took off either for the city or the Hempstead bars.

My parents decided to take the family to Palm Beach for the Christmas vacation. It was there I met a family friend's daughter, Nancy, who was to become my wife several years later. Nancy and I had sex, she for the first time and me my first female. I had no problems but found the experience not totally fulfilling as I did with men, but it was exciting. We had sex several times that Christmas.

I ran into my 60 year old white haired friend from the banker's party in Southampton and had sex with him several times. He had some "straight" friends and their daughter staying with him who were from Wesport, Conn. and I made a date with the daughter to see her in Conn. in January.

Morty became more effeminate and took to wearing makeup. Bobby and I excluded him more and more. I had two distinct wardrobes, one very trendy and the other very Ivy League Brooks Bros. Both sports clothes and dress clothes. This afforded me entry into society, Upper East Side Ivy, F.I., Village, and leather.

One night at Mary's I met a young man who became my closest friend and has remained so to this day. We were both 16 years old, our family backgrounds were exactly the same, and we found out our families knew each other. He was and remained the most handsome, desirable young man in the city of N.Y. through to the early 1960s. He became infamous for his beauty at all levels of gay society in N.Y. He was constantly receiving offers to be kept though he was wealthy in his own right.

I sometimes would not like to go out with him; though I was cute and good looking no one would look at me when I was with him. He became very pretentious but never with me, always being honest with me. John and I have never been to bed with each other though we have been to orgies together.

Nancy's family kept an apt. on C.P.W. (Central Park West) though their home was in N.J. I started seeing her. One night after walking out of the building I noticed a lot of seemingly gay guys going into the park behind the wall. I followed and was confronted with several sex scenes going on. I became a sandwich between a massive black guy and a blond. It was one of those frightening, exciting experiences that was repeated each time I saw Nancy in N.Y.

I now had the reputation as a desirable debutante's escort and was being invited to balls. John was experiencing the same thing so we used to go together and then take off and go to P.J. Clarke's on 3rd Ave. under the "El" where a lot of gays in our position went.

I drove up to Westport, Conn. with John to keep my date I had made in Palm Beach. John came with me as I had gotten a date for him. We both had never been to Westport. We entered a large estate with a private lake and heated boat house on the other side from the main house. We all went out that evening for dinner, a short dance, and back to the estate.

When we were driving past the police station we noticed several gays getting out of a car and John winked at me. My girl friend's parents thought it was too late for us to drive back to N.Y. and asked us to stay at the boat house. We said yes but we need some gas for the car and need to get it now as the stations were not open on Sun.

We left and drove to the police station and found the local gay bar across the road. We were picked up by two lovers who lived in Darien and were driven there. It was a strange scene that ensued. One of the lovers wanted to see his lover screwed by someone else. His lover knelt in the middle of the living room and John and I took turns screwing him. He had the largest, lowest hanging balls I had ever seen. They kept swinging and hitting me under my balls, which I found exciting and so did John.

We snook back into the estate at 3 A.M. and weren't seen. The butler served us breakfast in the boathouse and our girl friends joined us, then we drove back to the city and L.I.

"Boy did he have a beautiful cock."

Spring 1948 came. I was trying to talk my parents into letting me go to Europe but it was too soon after the war and Europe was far from being prepared to have tourists. My father decided to take a year off from work and tour the U.S. and Canada. My brother was away at college and my sister and I were old enough to be left home with the servants.

I finally talked my Dad into sending me on a teenage tour of the west. One of the first after the war. I couldn't wait for school to be over. Peter was becoming boring and we started having arguments. He wanted to know where I was going and what I was doing. He was dating a lot of girls and would go to Anthony's Bar also, then see Bobby and I leave together. Morty was becoming more and more strange. He started wearing his dead mother's clothes when he was at home.

Bobby took off that summer to be a councilor in a charity summer camp. My tour finally left. There were 25 of us, 12 girls and 13 boys from 13–18, the leader, his girl friend, and a doctor.

My parents left on their trip. We were supposed to meet in Yosemite Park and again in L.A. I teamed off with who I thought was the cutest, sexiest guy of my age, Paul.

The trip for me was exciting as I had never been on my own for such a great length of time. We went to Colorado, Utah, Montana, Washington State, Nevada, Arizona, Texas, New Mexico, and California.

I had had no sex for weeks and seeing Paul nude every night was driving me crazy. He had a washboard stomach and a full round ass.

When we finally arrived in Yosemite we stayed at Camp Curry and we were given a log cabin. Of course I shared it with Paul. I had gone horseback riding that day. Paul didn't want to go.

I got back to the cabin in the late afternoon, smelly, sweaty, and dirty. I walked in to find Paul jerking off. Boy did he have a beautiful cock when it was hard. He was embarrassed. I said don't be because so do I jerk off and just about every other guy does too.

He: "Oh yeah, you're just trying to be nice." I said, "Oh yeah, just watch." I stripped and started to J.O. He was fascinated and said, "Can I come over to your bed." Sure I said. I said, "You want to do it for me." He hesitantly grabbed my cock and I said just do the same thing to me as you do to yourself.

I grabbed his cock and he jumped. I said relax, we're just two friends having fun; nothing bad is going to happen. He got very into it and we both came and splattered cum all over each other.

93

Paul said, "I have an urge to kiss you. Isn't that wrong?"

I said why, there's no one here except the two of us and I don't mind.

He kissed me passionately and we both got hard again. Once again we jerked each other off while kissing this time. He moaned in my mouth when he came again.

Paul and I from that point on in the trip had sex two–four times a day. We would take our horses and go into the forest in Yosemite and do it there or under a waterfall, in a bathtub, at the edge of a stream, and in our cabin.

Paul learned to suck. We 69'd. His ass was so beautiful he was the first person I ever rimmed, which would always make him cum without so much as touching his cock.

Picked Up by 2 Men In Mexican Restaurant.

My parents arrived. Thank goodness I only had to spend one day with them. We went to the Grand Canyon, Bryce, Yellowstone Park, and Reno. (Las Vegas had not yet been developed and was only a small desert town.)

Paul and I sneaked into "Harold's" as we were under age for gambling. I had $200.00 and he $300.00. I won $2,000.00. He won $3,500.00. We left and didn't tell anyone in our tour what we did, but I decided I wanted to go to Mexico and would meet the group in L.A. when my parents would be there.

I bought a plane ticket but I could not talk Paul into going with me.

The plane landed in Mexico City and there I was 16 years old and speaking only bad high school Spanish. I was scared shitless. I had $2,000.00 in my pocket and didn't know where I was going and I didn't know anyone.

I got in a cab and was driven to a nice hotel on the Reforma. They never even asked me for my identification nor how old I was. I stood out like a sore thumb with my bright red hair, freckles, and fair skin.

I took a walk that night in what I was to find out later was the Zona Rosa, which is the expensive shopping and restaurant district. I went into a restaurant and was seated next to two very well dressed gentlemen. There were staircases with a fountain in the center and tropical foliage surrounding it. On both staircases there were about 16 violinists playing both classical music and Mexican tunes.

One of the men next to me looked very Mexican, the other very Spanish. I could only catch a word here and there that I knew but it wasn't enough for me to make sense out of it.

The Spanish one turned to me and said in flawless English am I waiting for someone and do I need help reading the menu. To the first I said no and the second yes.

Then the other said to me in perfect English with a decided Mexican accent, such a young man shouldn't be eating by himself and to come to their table—they would do the ordering.

I moved to their table. I introduced myself. The Spanish looking man was Carlos and the other Roberto. It was very hard for me to tell whether they were gay or not, as educated Latins never let their guard down with strangers.

We had a pleasant dinner. They then asked me if I would like to have an after dinner drink with them. They took me to another part of town. The street was dark and it seemed to be a solid wall a block long with a doorman standing next to a huge metal sliding door. The doorman slid the door back and there was an enormously long dim shiny black hallway and no sounds at all.

Once again I became frightened. As we walked all you could hear was the echo of our footsteps. Toward the end of the hallway I started to hear voices. We entered into what now would be called high tech— a glass, chrome, and shiny black plastic barroom filled to capacity with men.

Beyond that room there was a dining room with a huge glass wall overlooking a garden with a huge Jacaranda tree in the center and a dance floor around it filled with men dancing together. Whew; I let out a sigh of relief. They were gay. They told me they just took a chance that I was too, because of my red hair. They said they have only seen a few redheads and never met a gay one. They were as relieved as I was.

They were both in their early 30s and handsome but very different. They told me they were lovers, lived in Cuernavaca, and kept an apt. in Las Lomas de Chapultepec, a very affluent section of Mexico City.

They took me under their wing and introduced me to their friends. The next day they moved me out of the hotel to their apt. and had a party for me. I met Geraldo, who was a freelance store window dresser in the city. He originally was from Chihuahua and his father was head of the Protestant movement and he made a point of saying he was not Catholic. He was almost pure Indian and was about 19. His hair was straight blue black and his skin looked like velvet.

He spent the night in my rom. His sex was the tenderest, slowest, most masculine I had ever encountered. He had a muscular back with a deeply indented spine that I loved to feel.

I had always heard that American Indians were not hung. This was not so with Geraldo as he was at least 8" if not more and uncut but practically no foreskin. His cock was almost purple in hue, a color I had never seen. His pubic hair was as straight as the hair on his head. His smile was sunshine as he had beautiful perfect white teeth.

He had never seen red hair before. I had never been with an Indian before. We stayed in bed having continous sex for almost two days and slept only short periods.

I never really had sex with Roberto and Carlos but we showered together as they had a shower big enough for 4 with shower heads along the three walls and ceiling at different levels.

My red pubic hair fascinated them. We felt and washed each other and laughed at our physical differences and our mental similarities. They were truly loving, kind, intelligent, masculine men.

I moved to Geraldo's apt. for three days in a section that was a tropical Mexican version of Gramercy Park in N.Y. We had Carlos and Roberto to dinner every night. Our days were spent in bed having sex.

On the fourth day we drove to an opal mine north of Mexico City. I bought about 300—cost 24c total for perfect polished stones. We stayed overnight.

The next day Geraldo drove me to the airport as I had to get to L.A. before my parents. I arrived at the hotel to find that the group was gone for the day. They were out to Santa Catalina Island.

The phone rang. It was Dad. He said what was I doing there, why wasn't I with the group. I told him I wasn't feeling well and just wanted to rest and sleep for the day. They never found out I had been to Mexico.

The group returned and I got a chastening from the leader but he was afraid to notify anyone of my disappearance. Paul had told him I would be back.

I had dinner with my folks the next night. The following day we drove to San Francisco. Paul and I continued our sex relationship to the end of the tour.

Winter came and Morty's father presented a private detective's report on his son to both my parents and Bobby's parents. Of course it included us in it whenever we were with him but gave no report of our sexual encounters, only Morty's. My Dad threw him out of the house as did Bobby's Dad.

I was then confronted by my Dad asking me if I had ever done anything. I said no, that Bobby and I only went with Morty out of curiosity. He only half believed me. Bobby told the same story to his father. Morty beat up his father and put him in the hospital and ran away from home. No one has ever seen him since that night.

Freshmen Are Slaves For Upperclassmen.

My Dad announced to me that I was just too wild and he and my mother had decided that I belong in a military school and that they have entered me in one in South Carolina, where I will be taught discipline.

Since my mother's family was not too far from the school they would keep on eye on me.

Atlanta, the closest place, was 150 miles away. There was nothing else of any consequence close to the school.

Dad and I arrived at the large austere campus with many large brick buildings, all of which looked like 19th century prison buildings. We had driven for hours through vast empty ugly countryside, through poor dirt farms, cotton and tobacco fields. There was nothing else.

The town that housed the military school consisted of two blocks ending on empty fields on both sides. There was a feed store, luncheonette, combination post-office and grocery store, a small farm clothing store, a 5c and 10c store, and a cotton warehouse. That was all.

I could see my Dad's face drop but he didn't say a word. I kept staring at him, looking at his red hair and thinking of the night before, hoping he would say let's get out of here. But he didn't.

The main building was filled with young guys registering and some parents with them. I was assigned a room in "A" Barracks. Dad helped me carry my luggage to my room. I walked him to his car after we unloaded my stuff. I could see him thinking and trying to make up his mind to leave me there or not. Under the hot S.C. sun his hair was ablaze, his muscles were accentuated through his wet shirt as we were sweating profusely.

He got into the car, shook my hand, said write, and left. I stood there for about 1/2 hour hoping he would come back, then I started to cry. I couldn't believe he really left me.

I went up to my room and there were two other guys in the room who were my roommates ("old ladies" as they were called in the Brother Rat system, as I was to find out). We were told how that "Rat" system worked. We were assigned to upper classmen to clean their rooms daily and do their bidding at any time they wished.

I found out that I was the only Yankee in the company. One of my "old ladies" was a Charlestonian and I could not understand a word he said. My other roommate was from Columbia, S.C. and translated for me.

That night all the freshman "Rats" were told to strip nude and line up in the hallway. The upper classmen were lined up with only their pants on in the center of the hall with their legs spread holding sabres or twisted metal coat hangers. We were told crawl on our hands and knees through their legs, slowly. As we did were hit on the ass by the swords and hangers. The swords hurt but the hangers really stung.

In those years Southern guys usually were uncut. I saw I was the only freshman that was cut, out of 30 of us. I was embarrased to be different. My "old ladies" were not attractive. Wayne was fat with a tiny dick and Jim's foreskin was longer than his cock and was as ugly as he was. Jim spent the night crying and Wayne snoring.

The next morning we were awakened at 4:30 A.M. and taught how to make a bed, keep our drawers neat, and wash and clean our rooms. We were assigned to our upper classmen. I was assigned to a senior whose name was Merle. Seniors only had two to a room. Merle was alone in his room when I entered. He told me to strip nude and proceeded to handle and examine me all over. He said in his drawl, "I just wanted to make sure my personal piece of meat was all there. Boy, you'll do just fine, but how come they done slashed your meat. I ain't never seen no cock like yours. I guess it keeps it clean all the time. I gotta wash mine all the time 'cause it gets cheesy."

Then: "Now you damn Yankee, bend over." He took his sabre and hit the center of the sword with his hand so that the tip hit my ass. It really stung and I got angry. I turned and saw the bulge in his pants that wasn't there when I entered the room. I lost my anger and stared at his crotch. He turned red in the face and said, "Boy, you can put on your pants and leave for now."

"I loved to rim his pink asshole."

We were to clean our upperclassmen's room in the morning before we worked out and went to breakfast mess. When I'd walk into Merle's room he was usually in bed alone in the room jerking off under the covers; his "old lady" would be in the showers.

One morning I quietly opened his door. He didn't hear me and didn't have the covers over him and was whacking away. He had his eyes closed and I stood there watching. He opened his eyes and said, "Jeez, boy, how long you been standing there?"

I said, "Awhile, sir." Then I said, "May I help you with that, sir?"

He said, "What do you mean, boy?"

I said, "You can use my hand and it would leave both your hands free to do other things, sir. I'm at your service, sir."

"Boy, I don't have any classes this morning, do you?" He said his old lady would be back soon so he'd hold off till he leaves and I could come back from mess; then he would use me with no interruptions.

Merle had light blond hair, a sinewy muscular body, fair skin, smooth chest, a respectable 7-1/2 inches with a really big mushroom shaped shiny red cock head. It was thick and surrounded by blond hair and a beautiful set of enormous pink balls. His nipples were a real turn on. Even though he was fair, they were very dark brown. I couldn't wait for mess to be over.

I ran back to the barracks and into Merle's room. He was standing nude.

"Come on in, boy. Shut the door." He had just showered and smelled as clean as he looked.

He climbed into his bunk. I took off my uniform, except my Jockey shorts, while he watched. As I was undressing, I watched him get hard. I said, "May I help you now, sir?"

He nodded his head. I grabbed his balls. They were hard and taut. He said nobody had ever touched his cock before. I started to play with his beautiful nipples and he took my hand and put in on his cock. I grabbed his balls with one hand and jerked him off with the other.

He reached over and pulled my Jockey shorts down and grabbed my cock.

He said, "Hey, Red, I always wanted to feel another guy's cock and yours especially with no skin on it." Then, "I heard tell that some guys put their mouth on another guy's cock. You think you can do that for me, boy?"

I said, "I think so, sir. Let me try."

His cock was running with pre-cum. I took it all, to his balls. He arched his back, let out a large moan, and shot immediately, filling my mouth so much I nearly choked. He continued to have spasms and fill my mouth and kept his back arched. He finally fell back on the bed but I held his firm cock in my mouth.

He let out a "wowee" and said, "Boy, you's going to be the best Rat I ever had." I said, "Can we do it again, sir?" His answer was, "Sure, boy, and lots more too if you don't tell nobody what we're doing."

"No, sir," I said.

Merle became steady sex two to three times a week. We got into 69ing. He found he loved to suck cock too.

Merle's body was so clean I loved to spread his cheeks and rim his pink asshole. This would drive him wild and his pre-cum would flow so strong that it looked like he was having an orgasm.

Handsome Upperclassman Walks Naked to Latrine.

My company, "A" company, included the football team. One night I went out to the latrine to take a piss. It was late, as lights were out. One of the football players was pissing next to me. He was built like a bull, heavy and solid. I looked down at his cock. It was very fat but short.

He said, "Hey, boy, you ever been to a beat-your-meat contest." I said, "No, sir, what are the rules." He said, "Follow me and you'll find out for yourself."

We walked to the other side of the barracks, on the same floor where the football team lived. We walked into a dark room where there were 10 really chunky guys sitting nude in a circle playing with their cocks and watching each other. The only light was moonlight coming through the window. They made room for us and we sat down.

As my eyes got used to the light I looked at each one in the room. Boy they were big guys. I looked at their cocks. Not one was really long but wow, two of them had the fattest ones I had ever seen. They were almost like beer cans.

They all started jerking off watching each other and someone said, "First one to come has got to blow the last one." We all laughed and continued whacking off. No one touched anyone but I felt someone's hand next to me, hidden from sight, feeling me.

We all came within a short while of each other and cum was all over the room and us. Some of the guys shot from 3 to 5 feet. We all put our hands on each other's shoulders and said "good night good buddy."

No mention was ever made of these circle jerks but they would happen often, but only with the football team to my knowledge.

Every 2 weeks each freshman rat would have to serve hall duty for the night. We'd have to sit in the hall, do our studying, and monitor the hallways. Nothing extraordinary had happened on my first two duties, so when my third came up I decided to follow each guy that went into the latrine after 1 A.M. Nothing happened until 3 A.M., when a very goodlooking upperclassman walked nude down the hall and went into the latrine. I waited awhile and then followed. He was standing there playing with himself and was half hard.

I went to take a piss and he stood and watched me. To my surprise, he reached over and grabbed my cock and said, "Let me hold that for you." He shook it off for me, then got down on his knees and sucked me off.

I said, "Let me do the same thing to you." He replied, "Gee, I've been here two years and no one ever sucked me." He said I was the

100

first lowerclassman he had ever done because upperclassmen keep their mouth shut and he's had no problems. He hoped I wouldn't tell anyone.

He had a nice body, goodlooking face, and about 7-1/2 inches. Just all around nice. I never had a scene with him again but one night he burst into my room drunk as a skunk while my two old ladies and I were studying. He had a roaring hard on and was waving it at us. He went over to my fat roommate and said, "Hey, Fats, here, take it, it's yours," and waved it in front of his face. "Let me see that fat butt of yours. It'll feel good up there."

He then went to my other nerd of a roommate, who was nude. He looked at all his long foreskin and said, "Boy, give me some of that skin. We'll slip it between us. You got enough for two."

He then came over to me and said, "Hey, Red, here, take it," and stuck his cock in my ear and started pumping.

I gently said, man, we've got to study, maybe some other night, and walked him to the door.

I walked into Merle's room one morning and he was whacking off as usual. He stopped and smiled at me and said he was glad to see me that morning as his old lady had to go home because of a death in the family and he would be alone in his room for the next week.

"He pushed his ass into my face."

He said he had gotten some porno books and he read that guys can take it up the ass and get off on it. Do I want to try that night? I said, "Yes, sir."

I was nervous and excited that night when I walked into Merle's room after lights out. I stripped and climbed into his bunk. We played games for about an hour and then Merle opened some Vaseline and handed it to me. He got onto his knees and I was amazed—I thought he wanted to fuck me, but no, he wanted to be fucked.

I started to rim him and once again his faucet opened and the bed became spotted with his pre-cum. Was he amazing.

I rimmed him for about 10 minutes. He said, "Stop, boy, I'm going to shoot if you go on." I thought he was kidding so I continued. He started squirming and pushed his ass into my face and moaned. Neither of us touched his cock and he came all over the bed.

The bed now was wet. Merle stayed hard and said don't touch his cock and where is the Vaseline. He said use it, boy, now, and I mean now. "Yes, sir," I said.

I greased up my cock and his asshole gently, sticking some grease with my finger up his hole. He moaned with pleasure and said put your beautiful cock in me, baby.

I slowly pushed it in and noticed Merle was dripping again. As my cock passed his sphincter muscle, Merle put his hand around to hold me motionless for awhile. My cock was all the way inside him.

He took his hand away and slowly pushed back at me and I started to pump slowly. He started to move faster. I said I'm going to come if he doesn't stop. He stopped. I pulled out and he again jumped a little.

"Why'd you do that," he said. I just turned him over on his back, put a pillow under his ass, and picked his legs up and put them on my shoulders. He didn't know what I was doing.

I slowly inserted myself in him again. At first he grimaced. Then it started turning to a smile. His cock was once again spilling pre-cum. I played with his nipples. He took his cock and started to jerk it. I took his hands away and did it for him. His balls went up and down to my rhythm.

He started to cry out, "Red, I love you, I love you, Red. Oh, Red, fuck me, fuck me." We both came, almost at the same time. I finally pulled out and sneaked back to my own room at 3 A.M. No one saw me.

The school also included a 2 year college and there were 6,000 boys and young men enrolled in all. However, over 4,000 were G.I.s whom we had little contact with. Our lives were very restricted and regimented. Every moment was accounted for. I didn't even meet another boy from a different floor of my own barracks. The barracks were 5 stories high and enormous, built around a central court yard.

I was showering one afternoon after morning maneuvers. There were several guys from my company in the shower with me but there was one guy who I didn't recognize. I could see him glancing around at me and the other guys' cocks. I watched him get half hard. I waited until all the guys left and only he and I remained. He started talking to me and said he was from another company on another floor.

He was nice looking, rather average all over, and invited me down to his room, as we all had 2 hrs. to rest. He opened the door to his room and there, nude, sitting on his bunk, was a dark, curly-haired hunk covered all over in hair except for his back. He had so much hair only the very tip of his cock showed because of the way he was sitting. He had heavy thighs, calves, and ankles; huge muscular arms, and when he stood up showed a narrow waist, full chest, and broad shoulders.

Red's Balls Smell Like Perfume to Baldo.

I said Hi! He replied with an "allo." I said where are you from? He replied Italia. He turned to put on shorts and he had a round, full, hairy ass. Even standing, his cock seemed too small to protrude beyond his masses of hair. The hair on his head was curly dark brown, almost black. His face reminded me of a Roman god as I had seen in my school books. He had huge black eyes with very long eyelashes. Later he told me he had to cut his eyelashes because he wore eyeglasses and they hit the glass and were annoying.

His name was Baldo. Our eyes locked and he showed he was as interested as I was. He told me in broken English that he was from Florence and that his parents thought he was too wild and since there were no schools in Italy to send him for discipline (remember the war was only over 2 years) they had heard American military schools were the best in such cases.

So there we were from 2 parts of the world, in the same place at the same time, for the same reason (though I wasn't 100% sure).

I had totally ignored the guy who brought me to his room because I was so turned on by Baldo. As it would happen, we had maneuvers a week later and my company and Baldo's were teamed together. It started to rain and then pour and I couldn't find my partner so I opened my pup tent and as I was setting it up Baldo came running by. I said come on, help me set it up and let's get in out of the rain. We both climbed in soaking wet.

I said I've got to get out of these clothes and he said me too. It was impossible to move in the tent so I helped him out of his clothes and he undressed me.

I turned my back to him for him to pull off my shirt. When I turned around my hand hit his cock. It was rock hard and what was a very small cock grew to about 8 inches that had a thick shaft in the center but was thinner at both ends. It appeared to be like an oblong balloon. It has a flat, wide-lipped, mushroom cock head. It was darker than his olive skin, almost grey.

He was fascinated by my red hair and started patting the hair around my cock. I put my hand around his cock. The shape of it felt strange in my hand and very exciting.

He started to tongue me all over and said I taste clean and the smell of my balls was like perfume. He told he he wanted me to sit on his face. I did. I thought of that beautiful, handsome face in my ass and almost came.

He actually bit around the lips of my asshole. I turned around, sat on his beautiful legs, and leaned backwards. Our cocks were on top of each other. I took both of them together. We were both dripping and I jerked us to a climax.

I leaned over, pulled my legs back so that now I was on top of him. We kissed for about 1/2 hour and I fell asleep on his hairy body with his big arms around me.

His cock was only about 6" but even bigger around than I remembered. It took both my hands to go around it. He took my hands away and knelt down in front and started to suck. He made loud slurping noises. He was a great cocksucker.

He stopped and said, "O.K., little boy, you're going to fuck the best ass you ever felt." He covered my cock in Brylcreem, turned around, bent down, and put his hands on the bunk. I entered him slowly. I couldn't get through. He pushed hard against me. There was a pop and I was in. He was so tight it hurt, but it was a good hurt.

I started pumping. He said "Harder, boy." I was pumping really hard. My stomach was making slapping noises against that big hard ass. He was making "mmmmmm" noises.

He became tighter all of a sudden but he made no indication that he was cumming. I looked down and there were big gobs of white cum plopping on the floor. I shot my load, which he felt; a large shudder went through him.

It rained all night. I awoke to Baldo's mouth on my cock. I came with such force I heard him choke.

He started to jerk off. I spun him around and went down on him. The head of his cock was so wide I had trouble but finally overcame. Then I had a problem with the balloon in the middle of his shaft. I learned later how to slide my mouth to the root of his cock. For then, I could only go partially down the shaft so I used my hand for the rest.

I fell in love for the first time in my life. Baldo and I became lovers and no one knew. I'm sure he fooled around as I did. I still wanted Merle's ass, which I got whenever I wanted it.

"He was a great cocksucker."

The football team was in the shower room after practice and so was I. They were fooling around grab-assing and making motions of grabbing each others' cock without actually touching them. I watched to see who was serious and who was just playing games.

I noticed one of them with the beer can cock and massive chunky body was starting to get hard. I knew he had a room to himself as some of the football players had and I followed him from the shower. He invited me into his room, pulled down the shades, took off my towel wrapped around my waist, and said that "at that beat your meat contest, that was my hand on your ass."

He sat down on a wooden chair. He had a very wide ass, thick waist, and big chest. His body was hairless and hard as a rock, so much so that his rock hard big round ass seemed to touch the seat of the chair at only two points and didn't go flat.

We collapsed on the bed. I put my arms around this massive man and went to sleep. He woke me up with a big wet kiss and told me there would be another circle jerk late that night.

I went to Baldo's room to tell him, because I wanted him to go with me. I walked in to find him screwing his "old lady' roommate. He got embarrassed but I said I wasn't angry and jumped into bed with both of them. I tried to screw Baldo while he was screwing but it didn't work. Instead we made a sandwich out of his roommate. Baldo fucked while I got sucked.

The circle jerk was at 1 A.M. but we went to my beer can cock early to pick him up. I said to him since you're on the football team why don't you suggest a circle "jerk your buddy" night, it might be even more fun. I didn't really think he'd say it but he did, when every guy in the room was hard. These big masculine guys were first hesitant but then one guy grapped the guy next to him and there was a moan of pleasure. Everyone then did the same. Man you've never heard so many moans and groans. Cum was splattering all over the place. Not only did the guys put their arms on each others' shoulders after but every guy felt every guy's cock and balls.

The next time the football team was in the shower and I was there we really were good buddies and the comaraderie really showed. We horsed around but there were no holes barred. If you wanted to grab your buddy's cock you did. If a guy got a hard on in the shower we applauded now. No one got embarrassed.

We still had meetings in the hallways and the "Rat" freshmen still had to crawl between the upper classmen's legs but not only were we nude, so were the upperclassmen. Some of the swords, sabres, and coat hangers hurt but it was great looking up at all those asses, ass holes, and cocks and balls of every shape and description.

"He frightened me, but also turned me on."

There was one upperclassman that really was vicious and all the Rats (freshmen) got together, cornered him in the shower, tied him up, and took turns beating his ass until blood was running down his legs. We left him lying on the shower floor crying. He left school at the end of the semester and didn't return.

One night we had a contest of who could shoot the longest flame out of his ass from a lit fart. Baldo burnt the hair off his ass.

One guy had the most enormous asshole and another guy said I bet you take big dildoes up your ass. Big Asshole answered, "I bet I could." We got someone to get us a really big rubber one and talked Big Asshole into letting us shove it up. He took it all and got so turned on he shot his load while we were doing it. He squatted and shit it out afterwards to applause.

Bobby was writing that there were a lot of new places opening up in N.Y. on the Upper East Side and that the cruising was becoming great between E. 49th St. and E. 56th under the Third Avenue El and was I going to come home for Christmas vacation. I didn't think so because my family was going to be in Florida. Besides Baldo had no place to go so I thought the two of us would go to Atlanta for Christmas.

We were all lined up in full uniform that day as we were going to parade. There was to be a full inspection not only by cadet officers but also Army officers. We lined up next to our beds at attention and my cadet captain came into the room with an Army captain. I had seen the Army captain many times on campus and knew he lived above the 5-and-10 cent store in his own quarters on Main St. I used to think that he was goodlooking and always impeccable. He had a stern mean look to him and was masculine.

He lambasted my nerd of an "old lady" for being sloppy so fiercely that he frightened me, but also turned me on at the same time. He had the deepest voice I had ever heard.

The cadet captain stood at the door. The Army captain threw a quarter on my bed and said, "Cadet, that didn't bounce high enough. Do better next time."

I was trembling and he saw it. He bent over to pick up the quarter on the bed and at the same time told me to come to his quarters after evening mess.

After mess, I didn't know what to expect and walked over to his apartment. I started trembling again. He answered the door. I saluted and said, "Cadet ——— reporting, sir."

He said, "At ease, Cadet. Relax and come in."

It was the first time I saw him without his cap on. His shirt was open and he was barefooted. He had a lightly-haired chest and a mop of straight brown hair that fell into his eyes.

He put his arm on my shoulder and again said, "Relax, Cadet." He said that he never saw a cadet so frightened as I was that morning and that it's all a game and that he really was a nice guy and as human as I.

"Here, I'll show you. I have to take my pants off just like you do." He took his pants and shirt off, to my surprise, exposing a nicely muscled body with no fat on it. He said it's kind of warm in the apartment, why don't I do the same. I said I wasn't warm. He walked over to me and unbuttoned my shirt and pulled it out of my pants. I took my pants off. He said do I mind if he takes a fast shower as it's been a long hard day.

"No, sir."

He took off his boxer shorts and exposed the largest low-hanging balls I had ever seen, with about a 6" soft circumcised cock hanging over them.

"His ass was up in the air."

He said to come into the bathroom with my beer and talk to him while he was showering. I sat on the john talking, across from him showering, when he said to do him a favor and soap up his back. I started to soap him when he said to take off my Jockey shorts before I got them all wet. I did and started on his back again.

As I reached the small of his back he reached back, took my hand, and slid it down the crack and turned around to show a 9" hard on pointing up. He pulled me into the shower with him, embraced and kissed me, took my hand and put it on his cock. I took my other hand and felt his nipples.

We dried off and went into the bedroom. He was flat on his back and said, "Want to see something?" He took his scrotum and pulled it up and it all but covered his whole cock. When he let it go I grabbed his massive balls. They were like rock hard handballs.

We played around, feeling each other for about half an hour. I said, "I have to be leaving soon, sir."

He laughed. "Sir?"

He reached under the bed and pulled out a large wedge shaped pillow and turned over on his stomach on it so his ass was up in the air.

I started screwing him but then pulled out, turned him over the the wedge, and started screwing him again. I wanted to see that beautiful cock and balls while I was doing it. I jerked him off while I was fucking and playing with his beautiful balls. His balls almost slid inside of him when he came.

We were to have many fuck sessions until one day I walked into his apartment and his wife was there. I had never known he was married as his wife had lived in the Midwest.

Baldo and I went to Atlanta, made love in a hotel, and went to some bars on West Peachtree St. We were the hit of the bars in our cadet uniforms. No one asked us our age.

The year went on with lots of repeats of the kind of sex I've mentioned. It was 1948 and summer break came. Baldo went home to Italy and I went to L.I., N.Y. Baldo sent me a photo of a statue which he said stood in a square in Florence and said one day we would make love under it. He was killed in a motorcycle accident coming down a mountainside into Florence that summer. I was to see the statue he mentioned many years later on a hot summer night.

My Dad insisted I work that summer in one of his offices on 20th St. near 6th Ave. overlooking the church which is now the Limelight. I had several exciting encounters that summer with workmen, a black porter, and truckmen.

My two nerd "old ladies" from the year before did not come back to school and I was assigned a new roommate. His name was Billy. He was in my company the year before. He had a physical problem and I hadn't paid much attention to him. He was the "brain" of the company. He was going on 18 but he looked like he was 12 as he had a hormone problem. He never reached puberty. He was about 4'8", had a child's high-pitched voice and a child's hairless body. His cock did not even develop.

We all felt sorry for him. He became the football team's mascot and we carried him on our shoulders at games. His grades were the highest in school.

The first night in the room he told me he was all excited because his parents found a doctor who might be able to help him turn into a man and that he was taking hormone shots. He had his first one last week. He said the doctor said the shots may jolt his own body into producing its own hormones.

I really felt sorry for him as I could see him growing into a eunuch as an adult. He used to go to the library in the morning as he was physically unable to exercise with us before mess in the morning.

The next morning it was raining. Billy showered and left for the library and we were told no exercise that morning. Bubba, my new service "Rat," came into the room and shut the door.

Has Big, Hairless Body

Bubba was a southern farm boy whose family had a "gentleman's" farm in the mountains of N.C. He had worked on the family farm summers and was a big burly 6' and 190 lbs. He had blond streaked brown hair and you could see he could go either direction, either turn fat or become a muscular hulk. He was goodlooking but not extraordinarily so. His body had a great shape but there was a soft layer of baby fat over it. He was hairless. He came across as being dumb because he was so big.

I told him to undress, bend over, and grab his balls. He had a wide full ass and slightly wide hips. He was nervous and shaking slightly. I took my sabre sword and whacked him across the ass 3 times. His knees were now shaking. His ass immediately turned red. As I hit his ass it wobbled with baby fat.

I told him to stand up and turn around. He was quivering. I said,

O.K., Rat, this is how I want my bed made. He was standing nude. I said this is how I want my drawers kept and my dirty laundry is here for you to wash. He looked like he was about to cry. His cock had shriveled from a soft 3 inches to about 1 1/2 inches. He had a nice large set of balls pulled up taut to his body. He said, "Yes, sir."

I put my hand on his ass. It was red hot. I said, we're going to turn this baby fat into muscle, right?

"Yes, sir."

"Or your ass is going to be hotter than it is now."

I thought to myself that I would like to get into that ass.

I told him to dress and leave.

I saw a tear coming down his cheek as he left.

We had a hall meeting that night and as before the upperclassmen lined up, spread their legs, and had the nude freshman "rats" crawl through and get beaten on their asses.

Bubba was the biggest, best looking freshman "Rat." There was one new "Rat" that caught my eye as his coloring was so strange. He had reddish-olive skin, blond hair, and was hung better than all the other new "Rats."

I still was the only "Yankee" in the company and the new "Rats" were afraid of me because of my "Yankee N.Y. accent," as it sounded so tough to them.

Bubba was rooming with the "Rat" that caught my eye and two others.

I was still depressed about Baldo and didn't seem to have too much sexual urge. I was laying in bed one morning whacking off and Billy was in the library as usual when Bubba walked in. He said, "Oh, 'scuse me, Sir," and started to leave.

I said, "Don't leave. Don't you ever whack off too?"

He said sure but there's no privacy in his room with four guys there so he hasn't done it since he's been at school. I told him why didn't he strip and do it here. He said he never whacked off with another guy in the room, he always was by himself or in the barn.

He undressed. He said, "You sure have a nice one," eyeing my cock. His cock was hard by the time he got his Jockey shorts off. He had a fat 7 1/2" with loose skin that was behind the head. His balls were large.

"He went down on me but started gagging."

I said, "Boy, come here," and reached for his cock. He pulled back. He started trembling and said, "Don't hurt me again, sir." Bubba was uncoordinated like a lot of teenagers and whenever he

110

made a mistake I would make him strip and beat his ass.

One time I even put him over my lap and beat his ass with a hairbrush.

I thought to myself, I've never had anybody afraid of me and Bubba really was a nice kid. I got out of bed and put my arms around him and said, "Bubba, I'm sorry if I really hurt you and I won't do it anymore."

He started crying and said he was homesick, lonely, and I made his life miserable. I hugged him as he cried and kissed his cheek. We sat down on the bed and I held him. He turned and kissed me on the lips, which overwhelmed me, and said, "Thank you, sir."

We both had lost our hard ons. He looked down at my crotch and said, "Did you really mean that I could jerk off in your room with you?"

I said yes.

We both lay back on my bed and I started to play with myself. He watched and got hard instantly. We both started to jerk ourselves off. I was going to grab his cock but I thought he had enough traumas for one morning.

We both came and went into the showers together to clean up and go to mess. He smiled at me and said, "I sure feel a lot better. Thank you, sir."

I said, "We can do it anytime you need it."

One morning Billy came running into the room from the shower and said, "Look, look." He pointed to his crotch. There was some fuzz and a few longer, thicker hairs. His balls somehow looked a little larger too. The next week he told me that he had to go to the hospital for week-long tests to see if he really was changing.

He had talks with me at night, that he knew about sex but just never felt anything and what was it like

He got a hard on sometimes but it was only a morning piss hard on and it was pathetically small.

I told Bubba I would be alone in the room for a week and he asked if he could sleep there for that week as two of his "old ladies" snored and it would be nice to have a quiet night's sleep.

"Of course," I said.

The first night we were in separate beds jerking off watching each other when he asked if he could come over to my bed. Sure, I said.

He got up and tripped over a chair, knocking it over, making a racket. I said, "Damn, Bubba, when are you ever going to get some coordination."

He said, "I really do deserve to get my ass beat. Would you do it, sir."

111

I said, "You mean it?"

He replied, "Yes, sir, I do."

I told him to bend over and hold the wall with one hand, spread his legs, and hold his balls. I took my sword and with a full swing I whacked him. He just went "ugh." I did it 2 more times, walked to the side of him, and saw he still had a hard on. I whacked him 3 more times and saw his hand was dripping with cum.

I said, "O.K. Enough."

He turned to me and said, "Thank you, sir." His cock, hand, and pubic hair were covered with his come.

I said, well, since you don't have to jerk off now, how about jerking me off. He said yes sir and smiled. He jerked me off while he stared at my face and said, "Am I doing it O.K.?"

I said, "Uh huh." I shot all over his smooth chest. I wrapped my arms around him and we slept for an hour or so.

I woke up feeling his cock growing against me. I kissed him and we were both hard again. I went down on his cock and he came quickly. He turned around and went down on me but started gagging. I pulled his head up and kissed him again. I said, "You don't have to do that." He said, "I've never done it before and no one has ever done it to me and I wanted to do it for you." He took my cock and jerked me off once again.

—

"I started playing with his asshole."

The next night I said to him that he really liked me beating his ass didn't he? He replied yes now that he knew I really was his friend.

That night Bubba leaned against the wall, spread-legged again, but I hadn't asked him. His ass looked red and I bent down and looked at it. There were blood blisters all over it. I said Bubba I think you've had enough for awhile. I won't do it.

He didn't move. I spread his cheeks and looked at his pink asshole. It looked clean and I started rimming him. He cried out and wiggled his ass in my face. I grabbed his balls. Boy were they taut. He took my hand and put it on his cock. I pulled it away, stood up, and said OK, boy, now you're ready to suck my cock. He knelt down and started sucking.

His own cock was now dripping. He didn't gag this time and enjoyed what he was doing.

I came and he didn't know whether to spit it out or swallow it. It was running out the side of his mouth. I said, "swallow, boy." He obeyed.

He was now so hot I could have done anything with him. I didn't go soft and knew I could cum again. I pushed him in bed, turning him on his side, and started playing with his asshole.

He said, "You going to fuck me, sir?"

I replied I'd only do it if he wanted me to.

He said yes.

I lubricated us both well as I wanted his first experience to be a good one. He took me easily, laying on his side. He kept saying, "mmmmm."

His body was red hot. I put my hand on his cock and we both came.

He turned around and said he wanted to be fucked by me every day if we could.

We fucked in every conceivable position the next couple of nights. The blood blisters didn't heal enough for me to beat his ass until two weeks later.

Billy came back elated. He said the tests showed that he was starting to produce male hormones himself and though it wasn't at normal level it was increasing. He only needed an infrequent booster shot now.

The next morning he woke up and said good morning and his voice cracked like a 13/14 year old. We both laughed and I said, "Welcome to manhood buddy."

Every morning he would examine himself and ask me do I see anything different. His balls visibly increased in size and the hair really was coming in under his arms and on his crotch. His cock was getting thicker. His whole body was growing, as one morning his uniform didn't fit. In one month his voice became deep. A few hairs came out on his chest. His features on his face became coarser. He started to get enough peach fuzz to shave. It was a bloody mess when he did but I really was happy for him.

They discontinued giving him shots 5 weeks later. He grew 6 inches in 6 months. It seemed he needed a new uniform regularly. He started to exercise with us before mess.

The first week he exercised I could see he hurt all over and I gave him a rub down every night, which he was appreciative of. His body still felt bird-like, small boned, no muscles, but no fat.

Several weeks later he complained how sore his body felt. Maybe it was from all this fast growing he was doing plus the exercise. I told him to strip and I'd give him a rub once more.

Billy Has First Wet Dream.

His body now felt like a young man's, with meat and muscle. Even his ass became fuller. His cock grew to about 5 inches hard and his balls looked normal for his age.

It was amazing. He wasn't the same person anymore. He was a nice looking normal young man, although he was short. He actually was sexy.

One morning he woke up and told me his bed was wet, that he must have peed in his sleep. I laughed and told him he just had his first wet dream. He didn't know what that was until I explained it to him.

I told him jerking off to relieve himself is more fun and had to show him how.

That night he jerked off. The next night I told him I heard him and let's do it together. We did.

One morning he said he was going to go to the library, so Bubba came in to clean the room and we started fooling around. I was fucking Bubba on the bed when Billy walked in. He was wide eyed and didn't know what to say or do.

I stopped and said "Billy don't leave just watch." Bubba had his legs up and was jerking himself off while I fucked him. Billy just stood there and I could see his hard on in his pants. He said nothing.

Bubba and I showered and got dressed and the three of us went to class together.

That night Billy and I had a long talk culminating in me blowing him. He went to sleep very happy.

Beer Can was still in school and still on the football team. Bubba had been trying out for the team and Billy was still mascot, though everyone was talking about his change and he didn't make a good mascot anymore.

Beer Can said to me that I hadn't been to any of the "beat your meat" sessions this semester and do I want to come tonight. I said only if I can bring Bubba and Billy. He said he'd let me know. He later said all the team said yes.

We all jerked each other off but I explained to Bubba and Billy don't do or say anything more or they'd be in trouble.

I walked into the shower room one day and there was that strange-looking "Rat" with the reddish olive skin and blond hair and blue eyes. He was pulling on his cock and I said, "You ain't going to make it longer like that." He looked at me and down at my cock. I said "What's so interesting." He said "I was looking at your red hair around your crotch. You're the first redhead I've ever seen. What do you think I'm queer?" I said no.

114

He had that same indented spine I remembered my Indian friend in Mexico had and his uncut cock looked the same with very little foreskin. He was totally hairless except for brown hair under his arms and on his crotch. He was about 5'10", thin, and sinewy.

I asked him where he's from. He said he's a native North Carolinian, his father is a full blooded Cherokee Indian descended from the ones that weren't forced on the death march to Oklahoma, and his mother was Scottish. He showed both, with his hair, eyes, and skin.

His ass was kind of flat. He kept looking at my cock. I said you can touch that red hair down there if you want, it won't bother me or make me think anything different about you. I said we are all afraid someone's going to call us queer if we ever touch another boy. I said I know who I am so I don't really care.

He said not here but would I go to his room, there was no one there. He started to get a hard on.

In his room I took my towel off. He took his hand and started to pat my cock hair. He still had his towel on but his hard on was pushing it up. I started to get hard. He was fascinated.

"He put his hand on my ass and felt my hole."

I put my hand under his towel and around his cock. It was about 8" and not too thick. His towel fell off. I started slowly to slide his foreskin back and forth. He moaned a little. I bent down and started to suck. He moaned a little more.

I stood up and put my arms around him and all over his back. His skin was the same velvet I remembered from Mexico. I dug my hands around the muscles in his back next to his indented spine. It was the same as my Mexican friend.

He put his hand on my ass and felt my hole. I hadn't had a cock up my ass for months and his was perfect for me. He fucked me slowly and gently like my Mexican friend. His orgasm was so explosive he let out a large fart. We both laughed. I jerked myself off while he watched, fascinated.

We both lay on the bed and I said, "Well are we both queer or just two guys enjoying what we can offer each other?"

He said just two guys that fit together, and smiled.

It was now Thanksgiving vacation. Dad had business down south and told me to meet him in Myrtle Beach, S.C. as it was still warm enough to swim down there and he was meeting a friend and his son there.

I arrived and Dad told me to change my clothes up in my room. We were at the Ocean Forest Hotel in the better section away from the honky-tonk part of Myrtle Beach. The Cannons of towel fame had a small summer estate across the road.

I walked into the room to find a young guy my age dressing. He was the son of my father's friend. We introduced ourselves, got dressed, and went down to the pool.

We all had dinner together and my father's friend's son Jesse and I excused ourselves as we both had travelled from school that day and were tired. We both stripped and got into our beds. He was hung very big.

We started to talk across the room. He asked me what I do for sex in a military school and I said jerk off a lot and fool around with the guys.

He said, "What do you mean—do you jerk off together?"

I said sure and asked him how his sex life was and he said lousy.

I said what do you do then. He replied jerk off a lot while I play with my ass.

I said, "Play with your ass? What do you mean?"

He said don't you like to stick your finger up your ass when you jerk off.

I said no I'd rather put my finger up someone else's ass.

He laughed and said let's jerk off.

I told him to come over so we can watch each other.

He jumped into my bed. We started to whack away. His body felt good touching me. He was watching my hand work and he put his free hand under his ass. I said, "Let me do that."

He said, "I thought you were kidding before."

I put my finger in my mouth, wetting it, and felt around his ass for the hole and pushed it in.

He said, "Oh, that feels better than my own."

He turned over on his side and I fingered more.

I took my finger out and spit on my hand and spread it around and in his ass hole, spit again, and rubbed my cock with it.

He asked me what I was doing. I didn't answer. I started inserting my cock and he said, "No, no, don't do it, no, don't."

I pushed slowly in. He said, "Oh, oh, no, no, don't." I sort of popped in. He said, "Oh, don't move." I could feel his asshole relaxing. I said it's O.K. now, isn't it? He shook his head. I started to pump. He said, "Oh, that's good. Oh, more, more." I pushed him over on his stomach and pumped until I came.

My Dad told me that weekend he didn't like what my school was doing to me and was going to transfer me to a small junior college near the Main Line in Philadelphia, Pa. the next semester. »«

116

WANTS BELLY BUTTON LICKED.

We all have our fond memories. The first boy; even the first couple of boys; the large ones; the extra large one. Naturally we'd remember those. I am not thinking of them at the moment. I am considering the run of the mill blow jobs that for one reason or another stand out in my memory.

There was a young man I encountered under a tree in Central Park with the softest hard on I've known. Pulling it out and holding it in my hand was an unusual pleasure since I am always anxious to go down. I held it so long that the youth feared I was going to jerk it off and began to protest. In my blow hole it was also soft, but hard, and I got him off to his satisfaction. I don't even remember what he looked like but I still recall the touch of his dick in my open hand.

There was the bakery truck driver beginning his route at about 5 o'clock in the morning who would park a few blocks from where I lived for about a half hour in case I appeared, which I did whenever I could. He would usher me into the back of his truck where amidst the racks of bread, cakes, and pies I would suck him off, whereupon he would go to work and I'd go back to bed. I remember he was fortyish and paunchy but it's the setting of our meetings that sticks in my memory.

There was the youth who removed a mirror from my wall, placing it opposite my bed so that he could watch my performance without obstruction.

There was another lad in my sack who liked to pull his pecker out of my mouth just before he shot because he liked to watch me lap up the cum from his belly. This is not my preference but I do remember the occasions.

There was the young tough I cruised in a bar who took a swing at me while loudly announcing the presence of "a fag in the place." He followed me out with threats of punching the shit out of me but once in the alley alongside the bar only "made me" blow him. This incident stands out because sucking cock is one thing I've never had to be forced to do.

There was another who took me home, saying he wanted to fuck me. After coating his dick with one of the viler-tasting lubricants he changed his mind and I had to suck him off through layers of cold cream.

There was the guy who only wanted his belly button licked and his asshole rimmed and it remained for *me* to persuade *him* to let me treat his prick as well.

There was the guy who took me to his apartment near the park in which I cruised him. I left him well blowed and returned to the park, where about a half hour later I made contact with another young guy who proceeded to take me home to the very same apartment I recently left. This one also wanted his dick licked. There was no sign of the first guy around and I bowed to his wishes. Again I left and wondered for awhile whether I had serviced brothers, roommates, or what.

In addition to the memories we all have in common I am sure we all have these individual experiences that anyone else would have long forgotten. I know I can't remember any of these men as to physical detail but every now and then the incidents return to my mind. ✕

"GET OUT OF HERE YOU TWERP."

As for my brother, I put him way back in my mind as if he didn't exist. He has always been lousy to me from when I was a child right up to now. He has lied to me and stolen from my father and me. He is married to an evil Bitch and has two exquisite children, son and daughter, both bright, educated, and evil. I saw my brother only once with an erection, when he returned home from the Navy after the Second World War. He was whacking off in the bathroom looking at a girlie magazine. He has always been bigger than I in every physical proportion. It was 1945. I was 14, he was 19. I was hung about 7" then. He was 9" and fatter. It was not an unusual cock in any way and did not turn me on. Our Dad did though. My brother had and has broader shoulders, a hairier chest, bigger thighs, and bigger calves than I. I am 6'2", he is 6'4". He has very hairy legs. I do not.

If he followed our family pattern as I did, he probably is hung 9-1/2"–10" which he reached at age 25, while I am hung 9". His son is 6'7" and built the same at 26 years old and I would estimate him to be 10"–10-1/2". Whe he was born his mother exclaimed "I didn't give birth to a boy I gave birth to an elephant." My mother said, "his father was like that too at birth." My nephew's penis was always larger than most boys his age, as I used to take care of him and bathe him sometimes when he was a child.

My sister's son who is gay is 6'5" but hung normally at 7-1/2–8".

When I caught my brother in the bathroom after he forgot to lock the door he said, "Get out of here you fucking twerp." He only was nastier to me than normal after that.

His children are now "brown nosing" my Dad, their grandfather, in order to get the inheritance my father cut my brother off with. I'm sure their mother put them up to it. None of my immediate family has anything to do with him or his wife. Their children are two angelic looking blond blue eyed Germanic looking weasels. My nephew is an engineer/lawyer. He is a brighter bigger version of my brother. ✕

TEXAS BOYS LICK EACH OTHER'S SWEAT.

I read your books and enjoy the experiences that men tell in them. I am 25 years old and have lived in my hometown all my life. I am a homosexual.

Let me tell an experience from my childhood first. We lived out in the country near a creek and some woods. I had this time which is about 13 or 14 years ago. I had a friend named David. He had a better friend than me who when they got together would shoot BB guns at me. But when he came alone he was all mine.

He would show me dirty comic books like the one where Popeye eats spinach and his dick gets big instead of his arms and he fucks the shit out of Olive Oil.

Anyway we would get kind of horny and lick the sweat off each others' bodies. We were still kinda weird about each others' dicks but we'd spend an hour or so just licking each other—under arms, shoulders, necks, backs, thighs. But we left our underwear on even though we got hard and we didn't kiss. My arms and stomach would hurt from wanting to touch his hard dick. He had a little hair there and I didn't though we both had a little bit of hair on our legs but not under our arms. We had these licking sessions about 10 times.

He brought me many dirty pictures. Some we would find in the side of the road where old men would look at them and throw them out so their wives couldn't find them. He looked for them almost every week on our bicycles but sometimes it would rain before we got to them and the magazines would be bleached and dry and the pages hard to pull apart. He stole some dirty pictures from his uncle. One I remember was of a hippy with a moustache and a big, dark dick that looked so big to our little eyes, who was fucking this black chick. We would hide them in coffee cans and bury them to look at later.

One day I was playing in the creek bed with just cut-off shorts on over my white underwear. I was building dams. David rode up on his bicycle and helped me build more dams. We played with a GI Joe for awhile who was naked because I had lost his clothes by accident. So we played Tarzan. We got tired of this. He was only wearing shorts too. And he already had a little muscle but I knew this already having licked his chest in the treehouse so many times. But today he looked more handsome because he had been in the sun and was getting tan. I was still quite white.

Anyway we decided to be like Tarzans and run through the brush nude. We took off the rest of our clothes (our shorts and our underwear briefs) and we raced a couple of times back and forth through some brush by the creek. We were both getting a little hard and decided to see how it would feel to run hard. So we turned our backs to each other and made ourselves full hard. I looked behind me though and could see his white butt and the two lines on his dark back that point toward his crack. His butt was clinched and his shoulder blades stuck out as he made himself hard.

So he said "O.K." and we both raced back to the creek naked with our hard ons slapping our tummies making us hornier and horner as we ran. His hair around his dick was not much but smooth and black like his head hair. So we splashed into a little pool in the creek and I landed on top of him. Our bodies were under water from our little butts down. We slowly started licking each others' necks and David slowly started moving his little hard dick up and down against the bare skin next to my dick and I started doing the same thing. We rubbed harder and harder and licked each other harder and harder. The water was getting all murky and pieces of sand was getting between our butt cheeks and was painful. So were the rocks we were pressed against. We both came into the water at about the same time and real fast.

We didn't even know we were homosexuals. We just knew how to have fun with each other. He still came back to my surprise many other times and found many other ways to pleasure ourselves.

"I got hard just looking at the back of his neck."

I enjoyed remembering so much in my last letter that I decided to write again. This story comes from when I was about 15.

Once again I am now 25 years old. I am slender but muscular with brown hair cut short and green eyes and 6 feet tall. I have been lifting weights for 3 years and have a good body with hair on my upper chest and thick at my crotch but no hair on my round butt. I like to look at myself in the mirror in my white underwear as I write these memories.

O.K. The story: my parents have been good in the past about picking families with two or more boys in them to become friends with. One family was in the next town, which is small just like my town, but both of our families live in the country. This family had three boys. All were athletic and they all liked to swim but the youngest was the one who didn't have to work. He was about 13 and there was also the oldest boy who was 19. But the one I want to talk about is Derek, who was my age, 15.

I would go over to their house and we would look at their Sex to Sexty magazines and talk about girls.

One weekend the youngest, Kenneth, was at our house and we went walking by our creek. He was the tannest 13 year old I had ever

120

seen. The whole family had dark hair. He was very cute but my mind was so intended on getting Derek that that was all I talked about. I asked Kenneth everything about him. Does he have a girlfriend and all that. And I asked him "How big is he" meaning his dick. (We were peeing.) Kenneth's dick was small and white in his dark hand. But he didn't know what I meant and said, "You've seen him," meaning his body. And I said, "No, how *big* is he?" He still didn't understand. I also asked him did Derek have hair (meaning his chest).

But O.K. here finally is the good part. I was over at their house one Sunday and of all luck Derek was the only boy home. I had his full attention and he asked me to go riding on his motorcycle. Well I got on thinking he meant for me to test it out but he got on too to drive. He meant he wanted us both to go riding.

My stomach was hurting because he was so beautiful. I mean he was on the freshman football team, had dark curly hair and blue eyes, and because of the football team already had this great body that I only got at 19, but was not football bulgy, it was lean and had a little bit of tan left from last summer.

Anyway I put my arms around his stomach and my throat started hurting and I could feel a little hair between the buttons of his shirt. Of course I got hard just looking at the back of his neck.

We pulled up to a creek with a grove of pecan trees and lots of green grass. We piddled around throwing rocks and stuff. He suggested we lie down on the grass and take a nap. Which seemed weird to me. I mean our age and all but I wanted to do anything he wanted. So we laid down in a shade. Everything was so green. And he took off his shirt to lie on and told me to and I could see he had a tiny bit of hair across the middle of his chest and a lot more from his "inney" belly button down. Boyd I was in heaven.

We had not laid there long when he turned over on his side. Even though I had my arm over my eyes it was fixed so I could see everything and he ran his hand over my hairless chest and I moved my arm and looked surprised. Because I couldn't believe this absolute god was giving me attention. I mean I wasn't ugly but I was shy. And then he kissed me right on the mouth.

I still didn't say nothing. He reached up to move on top of me and I could see the little hairs under his arms (which is still a big turn on) and he lay on top of me as I started breathing real heavy. And the feel of his stomach hair against my stomach was too great.

He started moving his crotch up and down against mine. We still had our blue jeans on. And both our dicks were real hard by this time. He stood up and told me to stand up and we pulled our blue jeans and underwear down to our ankles and both of our 6" dicks bobbed up and down.

122

I was smiling and he started laughing, putting his head under my arm, and threw me to the ground to wrestle with hard ons. He had a beautiful tan line. His butt was so white and had a few black hairs on it. We bit each other, sort of playing, and let each other's hard dicks hit each other on the face, chest, ear, and leg. We both smelled of beautiful boy sweat.

And we bit each other. I liked to bite his butt which was so white. We finally got tired and laid back down to talk and while we were talking we slowly jacked each other off. Our blue jeans and underwear were still around our ankles and he was so funny as we sat there and talked and brought each other to cumming. He was so playful.

After we had wiped off we walked around awhile with our shirts off and went home.

Clinic Roommate, 23, Is "Straight" and in Heat.

Part of my reasons for writing to you in this way that I wouldn't normally is my parents called me home although I'm 25 as I said. I was in a clinic for alcoholism and this being at home is frustrating to me so I can write to you my rather clean but sometimes sexy stories. I'll try to be explicit but as you've asked I won't make anything up. Just the facts Jack.

This story comes from the alcohol clinic and is about a guy named Joe. That's really his name. Joe is from Dallas and he got in trouble at work for drinking too much and his insurance pays for alcohol treatment so he was there and my roommate.

Joe is about 22 and very smart, he's straight with a wife and new son. He has dark hair that is long but he doesn't do it up in the real cowboy/disco fashion with blow dryer. It's just sort of mushed up.

He's about 6' and has a hairless chest and real beefy from working construction jobs. He's got the making of a beer belly but not there yet. He has that well fed look with a tan chest and white legs which were kind of hairy.

Joe would go to bed in pajama bottoms and he claimed it got too hot for him to wear the pajama shirt. We would sit up late and talk on our beds and he would prop his head on his arm and I could see the beautiful fine hairs of his underarms. They were black and I would love to kiss them.

Joe was used to having his wife every night I suppose and he kept complaining how horney he was. He kept talking to me about how cute some of the nurses were and how he wished his wife would visit him so he could fuck her while nobody was around.

I kept seeing his dick get kind of hard and he would walk to the bathroom to pee and I could see it was pretty big underneath the pajamas because he didn't wear underwear either. I could also every once in awhile see the flesh of it between the gaps and the black hair of his crotch.

Joe had a strong nose and heavy eyebrows. He probably had some Mexican in his family but it was removed. He had a full face and thick lips and spoke in a deep joking voice. He was very hot.

One night Joe was in the shower and I listened at the door and could tell he was jacking off just by the regular splash of water. His two weeks would be up in a couple of days and I decided if I wanted this beefcake now was my chance. I barged in saying "I'm sorry I need to go to the bathroom." He was sort of startled but he was caught because he had a red dick about 7" long that he was kneading straight down with some soap. And he said something like "just relieving a little pressure." I tried to pee but couldn't because I was hard by now so I turned around and he said "come on if if you want to." I nearly dropped my teeth. I couldn't believe my luck.

I took off my pajamas and underwear with my back turned to him and jumped in to face him in the shower. I started by taking a little soap from his little bit softened but still fat gorgeous dick which he acted startled as if that's not what he intended. But as I moved my hand to my dick I moved my other back to his and started pulling it. His dick started getting harder again as I slowly kneaded it and mine and I said something like "now does that feel better" and he kind of smirked.

We did that for awhile and he let me kiss the small soft nipples on his big beefy chest and I ran my hand, still soaped, over his chest and he reached down and started slowly massaging my dick.

I turned him round and soaped up his broad back with lather. He had such a beautiful back and his big butt stuck out like a shelf and I ran my hands over it and soaped up the hair inside. Then he turned back around and I faced away from him and moved my legs in tight. Although the floor was slippery he fucked between my legs until he came.

"Then I slowly licked his asshole."

But we weren't finished as I thought we would've been. We rinsed off and then toweled each other off and he told me to get on his bed. We sat facing each other with legs crossed and jacked each other for awhile. It was beautiful blue in the room from the streetlight outside and he laid back and I started sucking his dick which was too big to put in my mouth. It was thicker at the base than at the head and not veiny at all but smooth. So I nursed it for awhile and I started raising up and he pushed me on my back and started playing with my dick to get it full hard again. He licked the shaft a little reluctantly and finally put his mouth over the head and jacked me off while I played with his beautiful black hair and stuck my fingers in his ears. Until I said I was ready to come and he let me come all over my stomach.

I've just thought he reminds me most of Tony Danza especially in the face.

So then I pushed him back on his back again and rubbed my come onto his dick and made it hard again. I started sucking again and cupped my hands between his legs and under his butt. His dick slapped on his belly as I lifted his legs up with his help and sucked on his hairy balls. The hairs were so long.

And then I slowly licked his asshole and the place between balls and asshole just waiting for him to relax and fart. But it all smelled perfumy from the hospital Ivory soap but I loved it.

After running my hands all over his butt clinching it and feeling the little hair at the base of his back I moved his legs back down on top of mine. And brought him to a climax by sucking him again.

I stretched out beside him flicking my tongue on his chest all the way up and into his delicious armpits a bit. I wanted to kiss him on the mouth real bad but I didn't. We moved so that I was on my back and he laid on top of me face to face. He had such a beautiful face and though his teeth were a bit crooked a pretty smile. His naked weight on top of me was heaven. I could hardly breathe. He raised his arms over my head so I could easily stick my nose under his arms.

I slowly trailed my fingers up and down his back. His biceps were so muscular. I kissed them and his shoulders. I traced my hands over his cool (because the air conditioner was on) and fat ass. Touching his asshole. The coolness made our nipples hard and I pinched his. He laughed and said let's fuck again.

So I closed my legs tight. Boy was he horney. He rubbed his incredible dick with spit and with an effort got it hard again and put it between mylegs. Before he started slowly pumping he kissed me on the neck a couple of times and then to my surprise on my lips. At first he kissed me hard and distracted but as he pumped harder trying to keep his dick hard he gave me a long French kiss. His tongue tasted warm, clean, and a little milky but smooth.

His crotch hair packed against my balls felt great. But he couldn't stay hard and finally stopped pumping but kept kissing me with his tongue until he slowly stopped.

He laughed and said he was a little tired so I got up, kissed his cheek and then his butt and then slapped his butt and went to bed.

The next day we didn't act like anything unusual happened. We took showers together again the next night.

Before leaving the day after that he gave me his address but I haven't written.

"He asked if he could lie down with us."

I would like to confess something before I relate something really good. Some of your readers my find this real stupid but I think most of them understand. When I was in college and even before, I had many tricks but I do not like to get fucked. I prefer the calmer stuff like licking and such. But I find fucking real uncomfortable.

This is the story of my favorite relationship. I was running around with several gay guys who were centered around one older man who was very funny and flattering. We would all go to his house and eat and talk and stuff. One of the closest in this group was my friend Kevin who I ran around with most. He was blond, not thin, but slender, and was very energetic and funny but not in a nellie way.

Anyway this older man invites us all—we were all 19-21—to his vacation home in San Marcos and we were all to invite a friend for the weekend.

Well Kevin and I had seen a boy in a bar who looked better and behaved better than the rest even though he might be just a little bit nellie but we couldn't tell. It was my idea to invite him but Kevin was backing me up. He was our type to a tee, clean cut, no disco clothes, no attitude, and a Ricky Nelson/Wally Cleaver body and look. So we asked him to this thing and he accepted and smiled.

It was all quite weird because we really didn't know what was supposed to happen. So we got to San Marcos and drank a few beers and played hide and seek in the dark in the house. People were grabbing other people's crotches and wrecking the house. Kevin and I were feeling kind of silly and were hiding in the bathtub giggling, hoping this boy Stephen would find us, and Kevin kept saying "He's so cute" and I was going "I know."

So eventually the game was over and everybody was little bit drunk. Kevin and I didn't know who Stephen wanted and we didn't want to be jealous of each other. So while everybody was lying around kind of drunk Kevin and I laid down on a bed to ourselves in a room with only one single bed. We had never fooled with each other before and were still just friends.

Well who should walk in and ask what are y'all doing but Stephen. And asked if could lie down with us even though it wasn't but a single bed. We said sure. Kevin and I were giggling like teenage girls and gouging each other. So Kevin kissed me and I kissed Stephen and Stephen kissed Kevin with me playing a very difficult job in the middle.

126

Well someone got up and closed the door because people kept looking in the door to see what we were doing. And we slowly un dressed each other down to our underwear, kissing all this time. It was great but very confusing. So we played like that all night long until sun up just caressing in turn each others' legs, arms, chests, and butts. Getting hard ons but just touching them through the fabric in our underwear. It was very beautiful like a classical painting.

When the sun came up, I don't think we had slept but maybe an hour. We decided to take a shower. So we went, trying to hide from the rest, from the bedroom to the bathrom. Two of us slowly pulled down the other's underwear and we were giggling and cooing. Because it was too weird for us to be serious. Somehow I always ended up in the middle.

Kevin has a slender hairless body, the most beautiful plump white hairless ass, and pink nipples. His dick is about 6" long and sort of thick at the base of it where there is a bush of dark blond, but not red, hair.

And Stephen has brown hair on a beautiful well proportioned chest, a round ass, and athletic, hefty, hairy legs. Both have handsome American faces. Stephen's is more since he has short hair and Kevin almost looks like an angel.

So we tried to take a shower but just ended up laughing and slipping. Accidentally letting our hard dicks nudge each other. Soaping each other up and concentrating on the more sensual parts. We all said over and over again that I love this and I can't believe this is happening.

The next day we all left for home but we were unable to be separated we were so in love with each other. and it seemed to me that Kevin and I were friends in mutual love for this boy Stephen and I don't know how they felt but I was loving Kevin as much as Stephen. Kevin and I would do things like stick pennies in Stephen's loafers.

When we got home we jumped on my bed because I was living away from home, not like now. And we tore each others' clothes off real fast and got on my bed. This is the first time we ever sucked each other. We sort of got in a circle and I sucked Stephen's dick and Stephen sucked Kevin's dick and Kevin sucked mine. Then we would switch.

This went on for over a week with us getting together at our conveniences but it got to be weird about who would sit by who in the car or in a restaurant. So I called up Stephen and we decided to be together and then we called up Kevin and told him this. I hope this story isn't too much white bread. »«

127

"HE GOT MY BIG LOAD OF HILLBILLY CREAM."

It's a rainy afternoon so I don't have anything else of importance to do so here goes with an episode. I had said I had kept a diary. Well I have off and on but it was too brief. Some of the men and episodes I don't remember. I sure wished I had set everything down in detail and then I could have published them myself as the Autobiography of a Hillbilly Cocksucker. I don't see nothing wrong with my episodes—they are informative, educational, scientific. People have a long way in going to understand sex yet even though the same things have been happening for hundreds of years.

I thought I would write today about my experiences of meeting with a couple of guys I had answered their ads in magazines.

This 40 year old stud's wife was out of town so he invited me down to Kentucky to visit. I got a motel room and called him up and told him I was there. He gave me instructions to undress and lie down on the floor and leave my door unlocked. I did that and it was about a half hour before he arrived. I was really getting anxious lying there waiting for him to enter.

He came in and looked me over and said I would be just fine and he then undressed. He had just come from work and as it was hot he was sweaty and smelt like a man.

The first thing he did was to quench my thirst with his piss. It was strong and good—no weak beer piss.

Next I licked his feet all over. I then proceeded to give him a tongue bath on up his legs to his ass hole. He especially liked and wanted his ass hole to get a lot of attention. His six inches of meat was real hard after I had worked on his ass hole and licked his ass cheeks all over for about 20 minutes.

I then sucked on his balls and then his cock before continuing on up to his nipples and under his arms. He then wanted some more ass work before I went back to swallowing his cock deeply.

He then decided that he wanted his toes sucked some more before shooting so I went down and gave them some loving and back up to his ass hole and around under balls and took his balls in my mouth and washed them off good and then I went back to his cock with my tongue and lips and I soon had him shooting his cream down my mouth.

Then we went out to eat.

My second man I met was out in Ohio. When I arrived in town I called him on the phone and he gave me instructions on how to get there to his house. I found the place and knocked on the door and he was just wearing trunks. He was a nice looking well built 40 year old man with the most beautiful chest and nipples I had ever seen.

We went into the bedroom and he told me to go ahead and get undressed. When he dropped his shorts he had about seven inches cut cock.

What he liked to do was have someone watch him drink his own piss, so he got a glass and held it under his cock and filled the glass with piss and then drank it as I watched. He drank it down like it was good white wine, which it looked like, but of course it was better.

We later went into the bathroom and stood close together and pissed on each other and I got some of it down my throat and it was strong but good as piss should be.

We then laid down on the bed where I went down on his piss drenched cock and his balls and I soon had the new taste of his cream to savor.

He then sucked my cock and balls and got my big load of hillbilly cream.

Well it's quit raining now so I had better get out to my garden work. »«

NEWS HAWK

by Boyd McDonald

A man named Michael thinks—rightly—I'd be interested in a clipping from the Newark (N.J.) *Star-Ledger* of June 20. It's a splendid article by Donna Leusner on Boy Scout life in the Garden State which fails, however, to explain how these incidents came to light— did the boys, as I suspect, rat on their masters?—and fails also to explain just exactly what is meant by "sexual abuse." Our legal lingo is so Orwellian that what the law calls "sexual abuse" many people more intelligent than our lawmakers would call "ecstasy."

Anyway, a 45-year-old former police sergeant and scoutmaster pleaded guilty to 35 charges of "sexual assault" upon eight Boy Scouts and was sentenced to 25 years in prison. An assistant Essex County prosecutor said the scoutmaster fed alcohol to the boys and "abused" them at his home, at the county police academy, and at two Boy Scout camps.

Another Boy Scout leader, aged 34, pleaded guilty to two charges of "sexually assaulting" two Boy Scouts and was given seven years.

That many Scouts do not have to be "assaulted," and want sexual relief as badly as their leaders want to provide it, and can be easily seduced, and are in face seductive themselves, is suggested by a report from Dee Sushi, whose Scout experience, among other things, served as preparation for the editorship of *Night and Day*. A Scout in Little Dee's troop sucked off a half dozen other Scouts in a Washington, D.C. hotel room and a 17-year-old Scout stood on a dresser and did a strip tease of professional quality, with high quality bumps 'n' grinds.

I've tried to get The Sush to write the inspiring details of this crowded hotel scene, but no luck, even though I've pointed out that of all the articles Dee is working on, this is the most significant. Perhaps a groundswell of requests from readers will convince Dee to put out by popular demand.

The *Native* has moved to bigger quarters and I am proposing to the paper's management that they post a tasteful sign outside their new building offering use of their men's rooms to the public; millions of men on the sidewalks of New York have to piss so bad their teeth are floating but most of the public men's rooms have been closed.

Management probably feels that such men's room traffic would distract *Native* workers from their deadlines, and it is a good point;

but it is also important that a paper keep in touch with the public.

A good paper has its finger on the public pulse; a great one has it hand on the public pecker (or in the crack of its butt).

I regard the *Village Voice* as the city's best general interest periodical but its "gay week" issue offered a clue why its circulation remains so small. Its principal article was a featurette on a minor fetish that is of no more interest to the general gay population than the fetish for Bass Weejun penny loafers: the marriage of gay men (to each other). Holy matrimony is all right for men who have nothing to share but their lives, but most men want more; all too often when prowling around for sex we find only love. Most men, I think, both homosexual and heterosexual, are fascinated by the compulsive promiscuity and debauchery of classical homosexuality. It is these obsessions which have traditionally been the true genius of the gender.

Blow Jobs, Et Cetera

The only blow jobs reported in the papers are those that end in litigation or death. *T.R.A.S.H.* reports the blow jobs that end in ecstasy, written by the men who had them. *T.R.A.S.H.* is $2 a copy, checks payable to "Cash," and can be ordered from D & W Enterprises, Box 292, East Rutherford, New Jersey 07073. Its writers are from all over the country, not just East Rutherford. Love is well covered in other gay periodicals; *T.R.A.S.H.* specializes in sex. Its material has also been gathered into book anthology form twice (*Trash/Trucker*). See ordering information at the end of *Cream*.

What brings *T.R.A.S.H.* to mind is a superb clipping sent by D & W of an article by John McLaughlin from the July 27 Newark *Star-Ledger*. McLaughlin does a good job of trivializing the Meese porn commission.

Seattle is Mellow

I have never understood why heterosexuals can't be moral like us. There seems to be a growing feeling that God is getting tired of them too and is beginning to punish them for being so dirty and low-down. A Seattle reader who is also a strong writer reached this conclusion before he read Professor Shively's similar evaluation in my previous column.

"I read and hear in the news about the drought in Georgia," he writes. "I also read and hear about the Supreme Court upholding the Georgia sodomy law. Is this just coincidence or is it a punishment from God for such blatant bigotry? Washington state has laws that protect homosexuals and a tolerance for sodomy that is the envy of many areas of the country. We also have a lot of precious, soothing rain that falls ever so gently, keeping our cities clean and fresh, our trees green and healthy, and our people fair skinned and mellow. If the Georgia legislature would just let God's natural design flow freely through its people and allow them to fuck whomever and however they please, maybe they would get some goddamned rain."

Typical Heterosexuals

"These heterosexuals!" a man named T. has written on a clipping from the June 11 Providence (R.I.) *Journal-Bulletin*, and I can understand his exasperation after reading the article. It's an Associated Press dispatch about Albert Lee Thielman, 34, who, according to court records in Austin, Texas, suffered heavy gambling losses, spent thousands on cocaine, was spending an average of $500 per month on nude models, and pleaded guilty to placing a bomb in the luggage of his wife and three children on an American Airlines flight carrying 154 passengers from Austin to Dallas. Had his family (and the other 154 passengers) died, Thielman stood to claim $2.6 million in insurance money. But the bomb exploded after the aircraft landed in Dallas and caused only minor damage, no personal injuries.

The Moral Majority

President Reagan and the First Lady should be ashamed of themselves for bringing up a son like Ronald, who's in the July *Vanity Fair* prancing around in bikini underpants with a tuft of pubic hair sticking out the top and who also writes for *Playboy*—what, I'm afraid to ask. It wouldn't be so bad if his underpants were pure white but they are red, which at least has the advantage of not showing the dirt (the encrusted urine deposits and embarrassing fecal stains).

The Joy of Heterosexuality

A Seattle reader sent a clipping of a June 15 *Seattle Times* article by a school counselor named Michael Cook explaining why he's against the county "gay rights" bill. Among other things, Cook claims that the bill would protect homosexuals who make passes, to use his vulgar phrase (I'd use the more patrician "grope"), in the workplace. The reader comments, "I don't think this guy needs to worry about anyone making a pass at him," and a photograph of Cook's fat head which ran with the article bears the reader out.

The Boys of Brisbane

An Australian now living in West Hollywood sent a cutting from what he calls "the trashier of the two Sunday newspapers in Brisbane," Rupert Murdoch's *Sunday Sun*. "Sodomy" is still a crime in Brisbane and the clipping is a Victorian account of a 36-year-old "radio personality" who was sentenced to five years in jail for having sex with an unusually large number of teenage boys. The article's vicious piety does not conceal a picture of the boys sketched by the defendant's lawyer, Tony Glynn, as street-wise sophisticates who agreed readily to have sex with the defendant. None of the boys, Glynn said, suffered from the experience; some gained from it; some enjoyed being in the legal limelight; only one resisted sexual advances, and the rest used the defendant as much as he used them.

But there was no reasoning with the judge, a cracker by the name of Mr. Justice Miller. The whole state of Queensland, of which Brisbane is the capital, is "Australia's constant embarrassment," the reader writes.

Sports: Swede Has "Baggy Shorts," Aussie a "Lean" Butt

Most sports writers, or jock sniffers, as they are sometimes called, play it straight and seldom mention the butts, bulges, and briefs of the men they adore. But Ferdinand Mount, covering Wimbledon for the July 5 *Spectator*, mentioned (what the other writers would merely have noticed) that Michael Pernfors has "baggy shorts" and that John Fitzgerald "has to stand so far back to receive service that his lean Australian bottom is perched in the linesman's lap."

Thanks to J.P. for the clipping. I don't read the *Spectator*, I suppose I ought to really.

The Moral Majority

M.P. sent a clipping from the June 20 Newark *Star-Ledger* about a typical cop, Walter Williams, 36, who served 12 years on the Roselle, New Jersey police force and has been sentenced to life in prison for poisoning his wife. In calling for the heavy sentence, Assistant County Prosecutor Howard Wiener said, "If the public loses confidence in the integrity of our law enforcement, our society will come to an end." The judge, Richard P. Muscatello, agreed; he ordered that the ex-cop serve at least 32 years of his life sentence before applying for parole.

News from the "Straight" World

In his July 15 *Village Voice* article about the July 4 gay parade, Richard Goldstein reports that "a sailor read the banner about AIDS funding and remarked: "Gimme an Uzi, I'll show you some health care." Mmmmmm; that sailor sounds available. If he were completely "straight" he wouldn't have to proclaim it in such an extreme way. But even if he's available he's not really worth shacking up with; no man who needs the help of an Uzi is. A six-year-old girl, given a fraction of the training our sailors have, could command a situation if she were armed with an Uzi.

The "Straight" Life

From a July 6 *Daily News* article by Cheryl Lavin and Laura Kavesh on readers' complaints about the opposite sex:

I was over at this guy's house for the very first time and I went into the bathroom. After I came out he walked in right after me, and I heard him say, "Oh, my God . . ." He came out holding the guest towel I had used to dry my hands. He was trying to refold it . . . He told me it had never been used before and he was so upset.

Love, Your Magic Spell Is Everywhere

A woman wrote to "Dear Abby" in the June 30 *Post* about her husband, Bill: "Because I refuse to iron his shirts, he refuses to help me with the maintenance of my car."

On the Word "Bitchy"

Men call women "bitchy," but the adjective could just as well be applied to men themselves. In the July 21 *Newsday*, for example, Denis Hamill called the new Duchess of York, the former Sarah Ferguson, a "sweat-hog."

The Joy of Heterosexuality

Ann Landers had a letter in her June 30 *Daily News* column from a woman who likes "dining solo. When my husband and I eat out together, I might as well be alone. He never says one word to me."

As Maine Goes, So Goes the Nation

Locals and tourists in Bangor, Maine, watch your step if you run into James F. Baines, a sexually disturbed teenager. He's already on parole from Maine Youth Center, where he was sent for the murder two years ago of Charles Howard, 23. Baines and two asshole buddies, who are still in the Maine Youth Center, attacked Howard and threw him off a bridge; he drowned.

Baines isn't the only one to watch out for in Bangor. Sergeant John Welch of the Bangor police department estimates that 12 to 15 robberies of homosexuals in the Valley Avenue area have taken place recently. Street talk, the sergeant says, is that teenagers in the area proposition homosexuals and rob them during what he calls their "liaison." Welch urges homosexuals not to be afraid to report robberies; Bangor cops have placed a number of teenagers rough trade in the Maine Youth Center, which must have an ultra-sophisticated sex life.

Howard's mother has filed suit for $655,000 against the three boys who attacked her son. They'd really have to hustle to settle that debt.

I hope the reader in Bangor who sent this information in the form of clippings of articles by Jeanne Curran in the July 10 *Bangor Daily News* will keep us informed.

MEDICAL NEWS:

"Penis" Secretes "Pale Fluid."

"His mouth opened slightly, his head moved from side to side more frequently, he moaned, and finally a hoarse, half-stifled cry emerged from him, as his entire body arched up out of the water, toward her, his penis entirely out of the water, full and hard in her grip. Then he spurted, three times, her hand stroking it out of him again and again, the pale fluid splashing on his chest and stomach, before he relaxed totally and sank back into the water, sitting down again, quiet, exhausted."

—Felice Picano, *Late in the Season.*

YOUTH SHOWS HARD ON TO FRIEND

OK Boyd, here's my "letter." I think this nice old-fashioned sex should be a welcome relief after all those ass-licking, glory-hole-sucking, and piss-drinking adventures that seem to take up most of the space in your anthologies. Remember the good old days when we wore a tie and jacket to visit the gay bars?

As a good Catholic boy (an altar boy at 11, a Boy Scout as 12), I took the church's teachings seriously and worked hard at not having "impure thoughts," much less with fooling around with that "thing" between my legs. So it was not until I was 14 that Nature finally erupted and I had my first wet dream. What a sensation! I didn't know whether to weep with shame or giggle with joy. In the dream I was wrestling bare-assed naked with a smooth-skinned blond Polish kid who lived down the block.

The first time I held another guy's hard cock, I was 15, working in a bowling alley after school as a pin boy. (Those were the days before automatic pinsetting machines.) Most of my fellow pin boys were a scruffy bunch, but one was a real beauty. Let's call him Ronny. When he wasn't looking, I would stare at him and think impure thoughts, but I felt that nothing would ever happen between us because he was older—all of 17—and was always talking about the girls he screwed.

Then one Saturday night when St. Paul was having one of its famous blizzards, the boss closed the bowling alley early and I headed in the direction of my streetcar stop. Ronny was walking along with me and he looked at the weather and said the streetcar would never make it and why didn't I stay at his apartment a few blocks away—his folks were away for the weekend. Fine. It was a cozy place and Ronny sat me down on the sofa and made me feel at home.

He went out to the kitchen and came back with a half a bottle of bourbon and two glasses. We sipped and talked and sipped some more until we were very relaxed. Then he talked about his latest girlfriend and how he wished she was there. He had something for her. What? I asked. He whipped open his fly and pulled out the biggest and hardest cock I'd ever seen. It was at least seven inches and uncut and he made it throb up and down.

At first I just stared, fascinated, feeling my six-inch circumcised rod throb. Then I got up my nerve and asked if I could touch it. He go said go ahead and stretched out his legs and leaned back until his cock was stretched full length and pointing to the ceiling. I grabbed it and, fascinated with his foreskin, moved it back and forth over the head. He was watching me close now and knew that I was really hot for that rod. Go ahead, suck it, he said. That shocked me and I said I really just wanted to keep my hand on it.

Okay, he said, but get that hand moving faster. "Here—I'll show you how." He unzipped my fly and pulled out my aching cock. Not bad, he said, and started jacking me off, fast and hard, and I stepped up the tempo on his. I would have come in ten seconds if we hadn't been half boozed, but now I knew I could last awhile no matter how fast he worked.

And for all his talk about girls, I knew he had worked on circumcised cocks before because he knew just which part of the shaft—just behind the head—to concentrate on.

It was sheer heaven for about five minutes. Then he started breathing hard and said, I'm coming. Me too—and I grabbed a paper napkin and caught most of our come as it gushed out.

We decompressed with bourbon and cigarettes, then went to bed bare-assed together and had another session. We slept after a while but I kept my hand on his cock all night.

The first time I sucked a cock was during World War II in France. In the Army—by now I'm over 20—I was trying to prove to myself that I was "straight" and for a while it seemed to work, as I could get a good hard on with French whores.

Blows Soldier On Troop Train.

Occasionally there'd be some playful groping of guys in our medical unit but nothing ever really happened. Near the end of 1944 they moved our unit from Rennes to Nancy in troop train. It wasn't a 40 x 8 cattle car but a hard-seat 3rd-class car with six of us to a compartment.

Most of us had tanked up on calvados before the trip and as the train pulled out of the bombed-out station at midnight we were dozing. The guy next to me in our compartment was a six-foot farm boy—Calvin—from Louisiana with a sexy rebel accent that made my nuts hot. I'd groped him one time and he'd said something like "Not unless I'm desperate."

Now I woke up from my drunken stupor in a dark compartment of a train that was jerking along the rails. I shifted my ass on the hard seat and next to me Cal shifted too. Everybody else was asleep.

I felt Cal's hand on mine. He took my hand and put in on his crotch, on top of a cock that was long and lanky like Cal himself, and really hard. I gave it a squeeze and Cal immediately had it out of his pants and I started giving him a slow hand job.

But he wanted more than that and he didn't have to work too hard to get my mouth down on his meat. It was uncut but clean and I started running my tongue around the smooth foreskin. It was a very amateurish blow job I gave him but he certainly liked it.

I still wasn't ready to swallow come, so when I heard him panting I fished him off by hand, catching the come in my handkerchief. Then he surprised hell out of me by giving me a big wet kiss. Then he hiccupped and in two minutes was snoring.

The first time I fucked a guy was in England, 1945. The war was over but there weren't enough ships afloat to get two million American GI's out of Europe in a hurry so the army set up a couple of "GI universities." I got admitted to the one in Shrivenham, about a two-hour train ride from London, where I'd go on pass every weekend.

And in London I found out that though I was a whiz with French whores, I couldn't get it up with an English-speaking female. On those London weekends I'd stay in Red Cross dormitories, which were just like Army barracks. But one Saturday night after payday I was lucky enough to get a room in the Strand Palace Hotel.

I went to the theatre and saw a hilarious production of *Private Lives,* then I went pub-crawling. I ended up in a little pub on a side street off the Strand and started talking to this scrawny but handsome young guy, a Welshman, who somehow had not been drafted.

The chemistry was right between us and at closing time I invited him to the hotel and he said sure. We had our clothes off fast and were in bed holding on to each other and kissing and groping.

Then he spit on his hand and lubricated my cock and rolled over on his side and guided me into his experienced asshole.

After female whores, I felt that I had come home at last. The feeling was so intense that I came after about 20 strokes. But my hard on would not go down. I stroked his uncut five-incher and he grabbed my hard on and said something like, "You poor chap," and guided me back into him. This time it lasted longer and I jacked him off while I pumped a second load into him and we both came.

After that night I no longer tried to make it with female whores.

Gets Fucked, Sucked by St. Paul Youth.

St. Paul, Minnesota, the old hometown, seemed tacky in 1946 after seeing New York, London, and Paris; but I discovered the town's one gay bar. It was a dump but I got to know some nice kids there. Sitting in a booth one winter night—cold as a witch's tit outside, as they say—with three other gay guys, I found myself spending most of my time talking to and looking at Artie. He had big blue eyes and didn't have much to say, but our eyes kept locking and my cock kept tumescing as closing time neared.

I was living with the folks and couldn't invite him home. I couldn't

138

afford a hotel room and didn't think we could have sex outside in an alley when it was below zero outside.

When the bar closed we all hit the street together and I headed toward my streetcar stop. Artie walked along with me. Just like years before, with Ronny from the bowling alley. And just like Ronny, Artie said he had a place downtown and fuck the streetcar.

We had to walk quite a few blocks to get to his place and the wind-chill froze me to my bones. He had a dump of a furnished room but the steam heat was on. And when he got in bed stark naked, his body close to mine was like an electric blanket.

We held each other for warmth and I said something to him like: I'll never be cold again. He kissed me than with moist and open lips and we handled each other's cocks. His was a good 6-1/2 inches, curved upward, and was harder than any I had ever felt.

Then he reached over to the bedside table for a tube of Vaseline and before I could say Wha he had my asshole greased and his finger halfway up it.

I've never done this before, I wanted to say to him, but he was so insistent and so expert and his cock so hard that before I knew it his cock was halfway up where his finger had just been.

OK. It hurt like hell at first, but he took his time. And though I won't say I enjoyed it, it was nice having a really sweet guy want my ass so much.

He came quick, like a rabbit. But then to show what a good guy he was he flipped me on my back and gave me a first class blow job.

We spent the rest of the night sleeping cuddled close and sharing body heat—and fuck the St. Paul zero weather outside. »«

"CAN I CLEAN YOUR COCK FOR YOU?"

SAN FRANCISCO.—I'm thoroughly disgusted with the vote in Houston (on gay rights), especially with The Reverend C. Anderson Davis, a black pastor who sided with the K.K.K. in the defeat of the two measures. I lived in Houston during the period I worked for the Southern Christian Leadership Conference and put my white body on the line with arrests, assaults, and beatings for the black civil rights movement.

This letter is about Houston, between the years 1954–1961, when I alternated between that city and San Antonio. For a few months before I joined the Air Force I worked in Houston as a bank messenger, which allowed me to move all over town at will. As far as I know the bank never checked up on me, so I dashed into various johns (especially J.C. Penney's) and theatres (the Onyx and Rex) for quickies.

Penney's downtown store had two active johns, both with glory holes. The first, in the basement, had three stalls and the young stuff usually went there to shoot their loads. The second floor john had two stalls with wood slat partitions and a glory hole that had been so enlarged that one could get a big fat ass through it into position for stand-up fucking. My first adult fuck was there (I had been sucking and fucking my underage friends at the orphanages and schools for years and getting same in return from them); a nice-looking salt and pepper guy—looked Italian or Latin—was in the other stall one early afternoon playing with a medium-sized piece of meat and, being young and hot, my hard cock jutted out when I took my pants and shorts down. The glory hole was so big you could see the entire interior of the other stall. The dark-skinned man stood and put his meat (in fact most of his mid section, navel to knees) at the glory hole. I sucked the tasty scum out of him in about five minutes of heavy sucking. I put my cock though the hole expecting a blow job but was surprised when my partner swung around, grabbed my cock in one hand, and stuffed it up his generous asshole. It was hot, wet, and pumping on my cock—better than any kid's asshole—and there weren't any complaints of pain as I drove my cock in and out and unloaded into his innards.

I slumped back down on the stool as he left and someone else took his place who I guess had watched our act through a crack. The new guy stuck his head through the hole and asked, "Can I clean your cock for you, kid?" I stood up and fed my softened dong into his mouth. Shortly he had it "clean," hard, and squirting a second load of boy cum down his tight throat. He got my second load in about ten minutes of fervent activity.

Exhausted, I asked him, or rather motioned for him to put his meat through the hole. But he said, "I shot while I did you." He showed me the last drips off his sizeable fat pink cock end. I stumbled back to the bank, drained.

I fell in love for the first time at the Onyx Theatre. A friend had shaved my pubic hair to rid me of my first infestation of crab lice, so I looked younger than I was. I attracted my first "chicken queen" at the Onyx. It was a traditional theatrical meeting—leg rubbing, hands on legs creeping up to crotches, buttons unbuttoned, hands on already hard cocks, fingers rubbing the pre-cum juice around the cock heads, hands slipping up and down hard cocks. Then he dove onto my cock, swallowing it to the root. My lack of cock hair drove him wild and he got my nut in just under a minute.

"He liked long, hard fucks.

He led me from the dark theatre and I saw how good looking he was—short (about 5'5"), with black hair and a moustache and sideburns. He got me into his station wagon and we drove to Galveston Island, way out on the South End, parked, and in the back on a heavy rug he got my legs up in the air and within a couple of seconds I was being fucked by my first adult cock. I'd been fucked by several teenagers with big tools, but here was a 30-year-old man taking me, mentally a boy but much larger than he, fucking me deep and hard.

He told me he seldom went with older kids and although it had been fun he wouldn't be seeing me again. It hurt, and I kept running into him all over town in his ceaseless chase of young boys. It hurt each time I saw him. Each time he turned down my requests (my beggings) for another session. His name was Oliver.

At the Rex Theatre I met my first serious roommate, not a lover but an occasional sex partner when the mood struck either him or me. He was into weight training. He is (and was then) bisexual. Eventually married, has four sons. He moved to Los Angeles in 1970 and I visited him a couple of times before moving to San Francisco. We still correspond a couple of times a year. When we met he was sitting in the back row of the Rex, about three seats in. I moved just beyond him and played the leg game, which led to cock holding and after the film to his apartment, where he fucked me with his hot, fat, uncut cock all night, pulling me off with his hand.

In the morning he asked me what gym I used. I didn't know what he was talking about. I told him of my work at the orphanage and on

142

the ranch; I was well built with muscles gained from work, not a gym. I stayed with him for three months before I left for basic training in San Antonio, more as roommates than lovers. He would bring his girl friend over a couple of times a month (and usually not get to first base) and the fuckings he would throw into me in the aftermath were fierce, overtly showing his frustration.

I met my first lover in Houston too, R. R had passed out a friend's bar in the late summer of 1959; I'd been out of the Air Force a couple of months and was hoisting a few Friday night brews in a mostly dyke bar. Charlie, the owner of the bar, was in no mood for drunks that night and asked me if I could take R to my room. We got him into my car after the bar closed and upstairs to my room and bed and I took Charlie home, getting back to my room about 4 A.M. I pushed the drunken R to one side of my bed and fell asleep.

In the morning R hadn't the faintest idea where he was but took one look at me; hangover or not, shed his clothes and jumped on my body, got my legs up and over his small shoulders and sank his big prick in my ass with the aid of spit.

He liked long hard fucks and gradually I grew to like them too, but that morning I wasn't much in the mood, having had a hard night and being drained emotionally, I tolerated his fuck but didn't get a hard on myself and honestly was glad when he finished. After a shower, I took him to his car, one of the first Volkswagens in Texas, and dropped him, thinking I was rid of a problem.

At six that evening I was thinking I'd spend the evening at home alone, but he showed up and I poured him a drink. His sad eyes, big, brown, doggy eyes, followed me about the room, and I knew he wanted a repeat. He told me he'd talked about me to his cousin, a cute but very nelly Latino I knew from the Pink Elephant bar, the gist being that his cousin thought I was Houston's hottest number (the first I'd heard of this tale) and most sought-after trick.

R wanted another session, and how could I refuse those eyes? This time we spent all night in the sack. I did get it up and off a couple of times and he fucked several hard loads into me. For weeks he pestered me, monopolized my time, until he drove back to San Antonio to resume his teaching job. Every other weekend he'd drive over to Houston and I started to look forward to our marathon fucking sessions.

Sucks Two "Straights" Off.

One of the off weekends provided me with an experience which I have yet to repeat—a joint sucking session with two strait (sic) friends.

I met them on a Saturday afternoon at Cats, the lesbian bar owned by my friend. We got to talking about the Air Force. One of them, Sam (the other was Joe) had been in the Air Force and learned his trade, photography, there.

As the bar gained more patrons, Joe noted that the women, outnumbered the guys about two to one, were hefty and asked if they were homosexual. I said yes and I was too. They looked at each other and I thought, here it comes. But it didn't. Instead of shock, or anger, or silence, they were full of wonder at my gayness ("gay" wasn't an in term then) and questions. What's it like, why, what, where, when, and most importantly, how. "You don't look like what we imagined a homosexual would be" one of them said.

We sat at the bar and had a couple of slow beers and talked about my life. Sam and Joe were friends from way back. Both Chicanos, educated, and keenly attuned to bigotry. They were the first two strait folk I met who were into rights for gays as well as blacks and Chicanos.

The "how" kept coming up and I asked if either had ever had sex with a man. Sam said he'd jacked off with a friend when young. Joe smiled and asked who? I asked if they wanted to see up close what it was all about. They looked at each other and then turned to me and said yes.

We drove to my place on Oak St. (now a freeway off ramp) and I poured them each a drink and asked, "Who's first—or do we do this together?"

Figuring out who'd go first took a bit of discussion and Joe volunteered—or rather Sam volunteered Joe. Upstairs we went, got undressed, and got it on. Joe was well hung, his big fat brown cock already hard as I sank about half of it down my throat and worked the other half with both my hot hands. After a few minutes I pulled away from his hot dick and asked him if he wanted to fuck me. How, he asked. "Up my ass," I answered. I got the KY tube, greased my hole, turned, and plugged him in. He took to it like a duck to smooth water. He pumped a big load deep inside me. We lay intertwined a minute or two and then showered.

He dressed and I put on a robe and we went back downstairs to Sam. I showed Joe the bar and took Sam by the hand up to my room. He was nervous. I took his clothes off him. He had beautiful olive skin, flawless. I kissed his nipples and he shuddered. His dick was an uncut beauty, only slightly smaller than Joe's. I swirled my tongue inside his foreskin and into his piss-slit, tasting the first of his pre-cum juice, then swallowed his whole piece of soft meat and let it come up hard in my mouth and throat. I layed him across the bed, his legs hanging down to the floor, and knelt between them. I worshipped his

144

cock with my mouth and tongue. He moaned in pleasure. All too soon his cock, fully extended, shot off back in my throat, too far for me to get more than a hint of its flavor. He came loud, whimpering.

Showered and back downstairs, I made coffee for Joe, Sam, and myself and we talked. Joe was married (his wife visiting family in the valley that wekend) and Sam was engaged, and they both seemed to enjoy that evening.

A couple of weeks later I met Claude, who was to become a life-long friend. I didn't know how young he was at the time (17) or I'd have shit a brick. He had a big, hefty body like me and a big fat cock. He sucked like a pro and really enjoyed sex—had more fun with it than anyone I know (much like me.) We 69ed and slurped each other's cocks with real zest.

Claude has a twin brother, Clyde (a Baptist preacher), and would joke about his efforts to get into his pants. He was never successful, but he was with just about everybody else.

We became "sisters," talking about our tricks while we had sex. R became an increasingly frequent topic of conversation and Claude, who liked him very much, told me to accept R's offer to move to San Antonio, which I did. I was working for Joske's of Texas and was able to wangle a transfer to their San Antonio store, next door to the Alamo. Claude had a 1956 Thunderbird and we tooled up and down Main Street in Houston cruising. If we discovered anybody of interest one or the other would drop out and foot patrol the intended trick. If nothing showed we'd go home to my place and sex out.

One night he took me out Westheimer Boulevard to one of his favorite places, near the reservoir. We started to trade off blow jobs but the mosquitoes were heavy and Claude hauled out a repellent which got all over everything and burned like hell. We drove back, holding our burning balls, jumping up and down in the car seats, avoiding a couple of accidents by a hair, showering together for about an hour, balls still burning, cocks limp from pain. We sat there in robes drinking Vodka neat, finally laughing like hell. Our orgasms were strictly deep S & M, but worth it.

I moved to San Antonio with R and visited Houston from time to time until I went West in 1961.

Last night (January 26, 1985) M (roommate) went to the Savages theatre with me and was pretty much disgusted by the jack off show; he's into action rather than watching. An ageing but macho Latino turned on to me and started to play "hands on leg" until M turned him off. It is nice to be pawed over at age 49.

One of the dancers I hired at Goliath's (Los Angeles, 1969–71) was 61—had a body beyond belief and a 10 inch fat uncut cock he could get up and swinging by thought alone. Unlike Big Ed, another dancer of mine, he couldn't come by mental power alone without touching it, but he shot a big load half way across the club when he came. Last night one of the stage jack offers, in his mid-forties, with a medium cut dick, sprayed his load at least 15 feet.

I wish I understood the physical mechanism which causes me to shoot great distances. In a strange reverse, the slow, dribble-style orgasms are usually the most intense, last much longer, and leave me more satisfied—the kind I get when M's been fucking me an hour or so.

I'll return now to my youth. In the fall of 1951 I fled the orphanage in Norfolk, Virginia. It took me several weeks to get to Texas. During the interim I spend a couple of weeks with my rural cousins in the western part of Virginia—the same place I'd spent the last two years of World War II. Young friends K and B had matured into 17 year olds. K was small, dark, and as good looking as sin. B was tall (a couple of inches on me) and rangy.

B's dad asked B and me to drive over to the next county and look at some forest land he was thinking of buying. B and I drove off in his old Model A (the first car I drove), which had been in the family for 25 years or more. B tinkered and kept it in running order.

During our examination of the land B stopped to piss and hauled out his long thin dick and stood back, hands on hips, as he sprayed a long thick stream. I joined in. By the time I was finished my dick had come up hard. Some men have a terrible time pissing hard but I glory in it. The sensation is at once painful and sensational.

B shook off the last drops of piss and continued shaking his dick till it got hard.

"That feels good," he grunted. He started in earnest to pull his dick.

"Let me show you what really feels good," I said and moved to his front, knelt and sucked in six inches of his cock. He grabbed me by the shoulders and started to mouth-fuck me, jabbing his long dick down my throat, choking me. I had to push him off.

"Hell, K can't take all of it either," he mumbled.

I stood and said, "Okay, let's try my rear."

He shook his head, "I ain't done that before."

"You'll like it," I said and pulled my pants down and leaned over the still warm hood of the car. He fumbled at my asshole for a minute or two, getting nowhere, so I turned, bent, and wet his dick for him. I put my own spit up my hole and helped him guide his long, thin cock into my guts. He sighed and pushed all the way in. I think it was the first time he'd buried his cock in hot flesh.

146

"I wound up as the meat in a sandwich."

He kept pushing in as deep as he could. My hard dick rubbed the warm metal of the car's hood—a strangely pleasant feeling. He built up speed. I couldn't hold back and shot my cum against the metal, tightening my asshole involuntarily and causing him to scream and shoot his wad.

We couldn't find anything to wipe ourselves with but leaves. As we drove back to his house he told me about his older brother, H, then in the military in the Azores, who'd shown him how to jack off.

I asked him about K and he went quiet. I reminded him he'd said K couldn't take all his meat either.

"He swore me not to tell anyone," he said softly.

"Did you ever fuck him?" I asked, already knowing the answer was negative.

He shook his head.

We changed the subject.

Two evenings later, the three of us took the old Ford to the drive-in. Crowded in the front seat, we couldn't help touching each other. K was in the middle and about half way through the film, being the brazen son of a bitch I am, after verbal hints had been ignored, I put my hand on his right thigh. I started moving it toward his crotch. He gave me a strange look turned to B and said, "Shit, you told him, didn't you."

I said, to defuse him, "No he didn't—I guessed it when I blew him, that it wasn't the first time he'd been blown."

I lowered my head and sank it into his blue jeans. I felt his soft cock with my mouth and blew hot air. I unbuttoned the jeans and them open, pulled the white Jockey shorts down, and captured his fat pulled them open, pulled the white Jockey shorts down, and captured his fat uncut dick in my hot mouth.

B said, "Hey guys, not here."

We ignored him. So B drove us out of the theatre mid film. B and K often went to the spot we went to that night; K would blow B and B would jack off K. I was hot to suck K and B had the good sense to realize that. Besides, his first experience of fucking my ass caused him to want to repeat the sensation. It was a warm summer night. We shed our clothes and both K and I sank in front of B's long outstretched dick, getting it hot and wet. Then K sat on the running board in front of me as I knelt on the grass. B stuffed his tool into my ass while I sucked K. K had been sucking B for years but had never felt lips and tongue on his own dick. He trembled; before my tongue could make three complete swirls inside his foreskin, he came.

B was just getting started and I was not even hard. I took one of B's hands off my hip and onto my soft cock. He picked up a jack off pace that matched his fucking tempo. K's fat, short cock gradually got hard again in my mouth. I was in hog heaven, being fucked and jacked off and sucking my two best friends from youth.

B and I repeated our scene a couple of times in the next two days.

K was dead less than two years later, one of the last victims of our senseless adventure in Korea.

Remembering K reminds me of a recently dead friend, Glenn. He and Ray were successful young professionals and lovers who liked multiples when I met them. I was parading my tight ass on Selma Avenue in Hollywood in the early 1960s. Glenn and Ray were a few years older than I. They were driving, I was trolling on foot in tight pants and Levi jacket over bare chest. Ray was driving and Glenn leaned out the passenger window and asked, "How much?" I laughed and said, "Free."

So much for small talk. Glenn moved over and I climbed in and we went to their home just off Western. Glenn, who was an architect, had done the place over.

I would up as the meat in a sandwich, Ray and I 69ing while Glenn with his large meat fucked my ass.

Glenn's rod was like steel—the hardest dick I've ever had. I was sore every time he fucked me. I was their only three-way trick that stayed friends with them in the years that followed. They introduced me to many of their other tricks and got me to do a porn movie. I've seen the thing once and my mouth is so distorted from the large prick I got stuffed in it that it's hard to recognize myself in that 30-minute movie of five kids circle sucking and blowing their loads by hand for the camera. I remember that the Chicano stud I was blowing in the picture was heavy hung, with a fat uncut beauty that took both my hands and mouth to get off. After the filming we had drinks and I coaxed Chico back upstairs for another session and got to taste a couple loads of his bittersweet, spicy cum. What was remarkable was that after I'd drained him a second time he wanted me to fuck his hot ass. His hole was tight and he was in pain but he seemed to enjoy it.

Ray and Glenn broke up toward the late 60s. Both drank heavily and it soon got to Glenn. His liver failed and he died one weekend in Palm Springs.

I am a sexual animal. My lovers have come to understand this eventually. To be gentle and kind to folks is an added gratification and one not all men understand. Women who enjoy being kind are getting away from it, but will come back.

I've had many sessions in many of the johns on campus at UCLA. I'm not sure how much more of this you want. From my diaries I note

1,800 men, but know I've experienced thousands more—the sessions
I had with one to 20 men every time of the hundreds of times I went to
the various baths before AIDS; the hundreds of park johns; sex on the
road.

Sex on the road in Amarillo, Texas, for example. In the early 1970s
I drove several round trips to the University of Arkansas for long
seminars I was teaching. I used to stop in Albuquerque, New Mexico
and Amarillo, Texas overnight, taking three easy days for the trip.
Only once did I trick in Albuquerque, staying at a cheap motel near
the "Old Town." I was in a small shop at closing time when the cute
Latino managing it asked me if there was anything in particular I
wanted. Brazenly, I licked my lips and looked at his crotch. He broke
out laughing. He herded the other customers out and took me into a
small stock room. We started getting it on and I mentioned I was
staying at the motel across the street. We put what clothes we'd shed
back on and headed to my room, re-shed the clothes, and fell to our
passion and joy of 69ing.

Unusual for a Chicano, he was cut, but had a nice fat dick, which
slobbered pre-cum over my chin and face each time I sucked his
ample balls. The latter really turned him on and he shot his heavy load
when I was trying to get both balls in my mouth. His thrashing
excitement brought me off and I felt his throat muscles contract each
time he swallowed a load. He had to get home for dinner (to his wife
and kids).

M (roommate) had an exotic experience in Amarillo about the time
I was making my trips back and forth to Arkansas. He met a nice
looking guy at a fast food drive in. M's idea of perfection in a blond,
heavily built, tall stud.

"Hey, man, wanta go to a party?" the guy asked from the cab of his
pickup truck. M was suspicous but horny. He followed the guy to a
private club full of mixed white couples with mixed nude dancers,
also white, on stage. M was the only black in the place and wanted to
get out.

The guy clamped his beefy arm around M's shoulder and said,
"Don't this get you hot, man?" M says he just winced, which the guy
took for a positive response. The guy continued, "Hey, I got a place
out back—we can get a real drink there" (only beer was sold at the
club). He led M to a small trailer behind the club. He handed M a glass
of bourbon and let his hand trail down M's shirt, undid his belt,
pulled the zipper down, and had M's big black cock out in one move.

M sat astonished as the guy took a hefty swallow of booze and sank
to M's root, burning his cock slightly with the alcoholic residue. M
wanted to fuck the guy but accepted the blow job. It takes him a very

149

long time to cum being blown, but the guy was into sucking cock in a big way (like yours truly) and took a full hour and a half to drain M's nuts. He thanked M, never removing his own clothes or even showing M what size tool he had.

Gets Sucked Off by Disneyland Janitor.

I got several blow jobs and fucks and one equally sensational rim job in Amarillo. I always stayed at the same place, as I had good luck my first visit there. The Western Hotel/Motel was a strange combination of modern, comfortable motel with an old, equally comfortable hotel, attached to one of the best Mexican kitchens in town.

The first time I stayed in the motel section I had a great meal in the combo dining room and asked where their john was. Told it was out in the hotel lobby and downstairs, I went and I was surprised—three stalls with gloryholes between and glory holes in all three doors facing the urinals. The room was neatly darkened with subdued lighting. I pissed and hurried back upstairs to finish my meal and pay my bill and went back down to cruise.

In the centre booth I quickly sucked a hearty load of sweet dessert out of a guy who just as quickly left, leaving the space vacant only a moment until a well-endowed Latino took his place. This guy, number two, I sucked with vigor for about 10 mnutes; he pulled back, slid down, stuck his tongue through the hole, wiggled it, and I stuck my cock through. My God, the sensation. Pow. I shot my load.

He whispered through the hole, "I wanna fuck you so bad." I told him I was staying in the motel next door. He followed me out as others took our places.

In my room we sucked each other. Then he rolled me over and, using spit, fucked me hard, very hard until the door buzzer rang. I got up. Juan went to the toilet. I angled myself myself against the door, revealing little of myself.

"Room service," said a young Latino at the door. He was even humpier, if possible, than Juan.

Didn't you order, sir?" he asked.

"No."

But he entered anyway, rubbing his crotch. His crotch swelled as he rubbed it.

"I'm sure you called in for an order, sir," he said. At that, Juan came out of the bathroom, laughing. "Miguel, you shit," he said.

The three of us on the bed fucked and sucked like animals. Miguel was hung as heavy as Juan, but uncut.

Like the guy in Irving's *Hotel New Hampshire* I'll suck and fuck my way through life, whatever there is of it, and enjoy it again by repeating it in writing. Irving (according to M) is a good cocksucker.

During the opening year at Disneyland (1954/5), I was there with a friendly "sister" named Manuel R. On Tom Sawyer Island were a series of delightful caves which unfortunately have been redesigned since to remove the quiet dark cul-de-sacs where I had an adventure. I went alone to the artificial island—Manny was after the ample rear of a blond stud and was making goo-goo eyes with him (Blondie wound up in Manny's bed). A short, freckled kid was sitting on one of the fences. He smiled at me and I introduced myself, as he did, his name being Sam. He worked with the pre-opening to noon maintenance staff at Disneyland and as a hunter-sucker of men knew the caves first-hand.

Sexual sparks were popping between us. We both knew almost at once the outcome (cum) of our relationship. He led me into the caves, into a cul-de-sac, and using a small key opened part of the artificial stone wall into a maintenance room. He ushered me inside and locked the wall/door behind us. He sat me on a low display prop barrel which was in for repair and opened my pants, freeing my already half-hard dick. His hot, wet mouth slurped all of it in, in one swoop. He, his mouth, tongue, and suction were part of an advanced cocksucking system.

I stopped him before he took me over the edge and surprised him by putting him on the barrel, pulling his jeans down to his knees, and letting his hard, fat cock spring up (he had no shorts on). I licked his crown, ran my tongue down the underside of his hot cock, and sucked in each of his tight fat balls in turn. He whimpered while I sucked up and down on his cock. He couldn't hold back, grabbed me by the shoulders, and pushed me down to catch his heavy load. He held me down so tightly I barely tasted his cream.

"I alternated sucking both their cocks."

He soaked his cock in my mouth. It stayed hard. I tongued it. He eventually stood, got a clean drop cloth, spread it out, and we 69ed. He came again with the same whimpering passion and sucked another load out of me.

Sam told me about the use he made of the caves and his maintenance room. He said that I was one of the few that had sucked him in return.

In later years Disneyland tried to dissuade gay folks, threw out a couple of dancers, and so forth. For several years I looked for Sam but didn't see him again.

151

I spent a few weeks in Ottumwa, Iowa in 1961 working at the tobacco counter of Asco Drugs. I did two straits one evening (together). I met them as I was closing the store. Both were workers at the local beef packing plant and had come off duty looking for Copenhagen snuff. We were down to one can on the counter and they waited while I rummaged in the back room for more. They were humps— cousins of Polish descent with joyful, bubbling personalities.

We got to kidding around. I gave them a couple of extra tins gratis for being patient and they invited me to share their beer. We drove in their old Ford out to River Park and swilled beer, me in the middle. We told bawdy jokes, getting down and dirty 1960s style before the uproar at Berkeley, before Jack and Martin and Bobby and Nam lost us our innocence.

We got high on beer and horny from the jokes. Pol and Ignac (Iggy), my age, laughed easily with me. They asked if I knew any whores. They'd not been in Ottumwa much longer than I. I knew no whores but I said, "When I get hot I use Miss Five Fingers." Pol looked at me a bit funny. Then slowly it came to him and he burst out laughing. He said, "Iggy has to use Miss Ten Fingers for his dick. He's the size of that cannon." He referred to the World War I monument in the park. "Show him your cannon, Iggy," Pol said.

Iggy may have been shy about most things but his dick wasn't one of them. He whipped out his big piece of meat. "Wanna feel it?" he asked.

I started to jack it off. This caused Pol to laugh again. He pulled his work pants open and hauled out his meat, also sizeable. I followed and all three of us worked on our own tools. Iggy threw back his head and sprayed the dashboard with a big wad. It took Pol and me longer. I came onto my stomach and Pol all over his pants, which caused him to laugh again.

We got our clothes in order and drove to the small duplex they shared. Inside we swilled more beer. Pol rubbed his crotch each time he came out of the john after pissing. After one trip he came out with a hard on outlined down his cum-stained pants. I felt of it and Iggy took his cock out and started to jack off while he watched me rub Pol's hard on through his pants. I told Iggy to move over to the couch, sat him down, and sucked in about a third of his meat while I unbuttoned Pol's pants. I alternated sucking both their cocks. As before, Iggy quickly squirted a heavy load, this time down my throat, not onto the dashboard. It was spicy. Pol grew excited, thrashing around, and as Iggy watched my work he got a hard on again. Pol shot a lighter, sweeter load than Iggy.

I left Ottumwa less than a week later and I didn't get to repeat another Friday night with my Polish friends.

From October, 1961 through early 1962 I worked as night manager of the Keno game at the Nevada Club Lodge. I lived at the worker hostels the Lodge owned. The individual rooms, eight to a floor, shared four bathrooms, allowing me to see various occupants in all states of undress. I have slept nude ever since I was a kid and one afternoon I woke up, had to piss, and went into my shared john sporting a piss hard. It jutted out in front of me as I walked.

Arrested for Sucking Cock.

Tommy B., who lived in the next room, was on the toilet jacking off. I'd only seen his cock soft, and God was he a grower. From his small nubbin had come a mighty, meaty 8" prick.

He stopped jacking off when I came in and stared at my cock open-mouthed. I walked and stood in front of him, my cock bobbing up and down. His touch was light and tentative as he rubbed his pre-cum greased fingers on my pole. I let him explore my cock and balls for a minute. Then I sank to my knees and took a sizeable portion of his meat in my mouth. He sighed, leaned back, and let me suck him off. He jacked me off and then got into the shower.

Two afternoons later he knocked on my door, waking me. "Can we do it again?" he said.

I let him in. He took off his towel. I laid him back on the bed and started to suck him. He pulled me around and started to 69. He was amateurish; his teeth scraped my cock. I mentally gritted my teeth and let him learn by experience to suck cock.

He was a quick study, learning from multiple actions I was performing on his cock. He started using his tongue as I used mine and used his mouth to caress and we brought each other off. In the months I had left there we became a steady pair.

I sucked another resident (Mike) who lived on the floor a couple of times, enjoying his long cock, especially when he shot his wad, but I was only another hot hole for his fruity cum—a hole of last resort.

I spent two stays in Washington D.C., February–July 1, 1976 and March–August 1977. I was in D.C. to computerize government records and simplify formats and of course to suck cock. My favorite place was the john at the very end (South East) of Potomac Park. The john gave me many hours of pleasure. It had two stalls and two glory holes.

Most of the sex I had there was one-on-one and mutual, with black men. I estimate I had 250 in 1976 (and was had an equal number of times) and 300 in 1977. There were so many, only a few stand out, like an older man with snow white cock hair on the deepest black skin. He had a fat, uncut, iron-hard dick which rewarded me with two bitter-sweet loads. In between, he got a load of mine.

One lunch time in mid-week I entered the john. Both stools were occupied and a young black man was at the urinals. His cock was wet and hard, just pulled from the nearby glory hole. He watched me get hard and as he started to return to the glory hole I touched his hand and sank to my knees, mouth open. He plugged my scum-sucking hole with his fat brown meat. It took a lot of sucking to bring him off. The other two black guys came off the stools to watch. They alternated sucking each other. They both shot well before my young man. One of them came to my side and jacked my cock off as I sucked. Finally the guy bent down over me and shot one of the biggest loads I've ever gotten. The excess dribbled from my mouth.

The following year, sometime in June, they replaced the stall walls, killing the wooden glory holes with steel. In late July I was arrested there sucking cock in front of the urinals—arrested by three white D.C. Park police. It was that night that I learned what power was, and that I could wield it in the phony justice system in the United States. I told the police to call their government computer center and tell them that if I and my friend weren't freed by 8 A.M. I would publish the entry keys into the systems I'd designed (this is the plot of *War Games*). All hell broke loose. By midnight a half dozen F.B.I. types had taken me out of D.C. custody almost by force, along with all paper work—finger prints, pictures. The guy I was sucking when I was arrested was let go and told to go home and say nothing, and stay away from that john because it was bugged. He stood there on Connecticut watching me being hustled into a limo.

I was taken to the new F.B.I. HQ and questioned until 8 A.M. I refused to answer most of the questions. They wanted to know where I had hidden the code and what I intended to do with it. I asked them to review my record, the civil rights arrests in 1969s, the report from various folk that I am gay, which I told them is true. This seemed to both bug and surprise them. We reached a compromise and the issue was resolved when I told them I'd return to California and stay out of states where I couldn't legally practice my lifestyle and would not use or release the code if they didn't bother me. I hadn't really hid the code, but I very quickly did after this.

Sucks 2 Hawaiians Off On Beach.

So much for justice. Power talks, not justice. All our pretensions of freedom, etc. are all empty phrases "full of sound and fury, signifying nothing."

I lived in the Oakdale Complex, built by the Watergate Co., both times in Washington. Early in the 1977 stay I was in the heated pool. It was sunny but cold, about 37°. Another hearty soul, another beefy blond, another Californian, joined me in doing laps in the pool. Tired, happy, keeping down in the heated water out of the cold, we exchanged introductions. I ran back to my apartment, got a fire going, and was almost dry and warm when my buzzer rang. Jeff the California Golden Boy was standing there wet and shivering with a couple of bottles of Reisling.

He shed his suit and threw himself down in front of the fireplace, stretching his lanky body to get warm. I poured us each a glass of wine, dropped my robe in the kitchen and joined him in front of the fire. We sipped the wine, laying opposite each other. Our cocks got hard without touching and we got into each other's arms.

He got my legs up in the air and plugged into my ass with his big dick. Unfortunately, he only got started before he popped his load. He lowered my legs and sucked me off. The second fuck took much longer and his fat prick was perfect for my needs, causing me to unload all over my stomach.

It took us the entire weekend to finish the wine. Jeff was only passing through, working for some "quiet" government agency on his way to the Mid-East.

I met several nice guys under the various bridges of the Potomac. Memorial Bridge was my favorite; it was the haunt of political black gay men, being so near the Lincoln Memorial. The folks I met there talked about their political frustrations. I was among a minority of white gays in D.C. who enjoyed sex with black men. The gay ghetto in south east D.C. seldom allowed blacks to even enter their premises. I toured those bigoted locales once, taking note of the bigotry, never going back (or being allowed back after the questions and scenes I caused).

One weekend during a three-month project for the City and County of Honolulu in 1979, I drove my car around the entire island. Just north of Makaha I met two beautiful swimmers, native Hawaiians. I joined them nude in the water and on the beach I sucked both of them off. If only the world could adopt their laid-back sensuality, the popes and the Reverend Foulmouths would be out of business overnight.

I still go to the steam room of my health club, but sex is a no-no during AIDS, except for jacking off. Tuesday I had a nice jack off session with Ron, a nice old guy, white haired but humpy, and a tourist, George, visiting from Washington, D.C. George wanted to get more active but Ron and I held him to a nice three-way jack off. George is a nice big humpy guy with a fat 9" dick. Ron and I took turns manhandling George's big joint.

Wednesday the Chicano I've been making eyes at, the one who rides the "N" line into San Francisco, followed me down to the terminal john. From the first few mornings in December when he noticed me and hatefully glared back at me to Wednesday's involvement is a long path. Most folk don't take time to follow through on a prospective trick. This is especially true in San Francisco, where there are so many opportunities that sustained efforts are seldom made. Wednesday, no longer scowling at me, my Latin bus rider followed me to the Eastbay Terminal john. At the urinals, recently changed by the addition of small partitions, he moved a couple down from me, making quick little glances in my direction. I pulled back a bit to show him my hardening dick. He was self conscious. I couldn't see his. In the early morning (6:30 A.M.) no one else was in the john so I moved down next to him and looked over the partition. He was pulling his tight foreskin over the head of a fat brown dick.

5 Hours in a Bus Station Toilet.

I whispered, "Do you have someplace we can go?"

He smiled, stuffed his fat meat into his worn jeans, and said, "Yeah man, I work maintenance across the street."

I followed him out of the john, across the street, into the Fremont Tower, and to the second floor. He opened an unmarked door leading into a storage room. The door locked behind us. Clothes were shed—fast. I moved Juan to a low shelf and played with his fat, hard, and very hot cock—too hot. I'd just started hand work and was chewing on his big hot balls one after the other when he gave a little yelp and sprayed a heavy load over my face and hair.

Juan didn't lose his hard on. He played with my cock and balls but got more and more interested in my big butt. He moved me around, running his fat slimy meat between my cheeks. I pulled away, grabbed my jacket, and took a rubber out of my pocket and pulled it over his crown and down on his cock. It surprised him but didn't slow his activity. With the greased rubber easing the way, he pushed his cock to the hilt up my ass. I shivered with sensation.

He came almost as quickly the second time. I sucked his nipples and balls and ran my tongue down his stomach and legs, trying to lead him to a third cum. But time intervened and I said goodbye and headed across the Bay to teach my classes at UC Berkeley.

Other bus terminals have played a major role in my sexual history. The first I remember in heavy use—by me—was the Trailways Terminal in San Antonio, Texas. It was by all standards a classic. Two stalls, open, never doored, and two urinals and one sink in a very small room. There were square-cut glory holes, 3" by 3", between the stalls and the urinals. I worked two blocks away at an engineering firm and made my tea breaks at said bus john when able. Almost every afternoon (and as well at lunch time) there was activity in this john.

The very first time I went there I went to the vacant stall, looked through the hole facing the urinals, and saw a pair of pants and a hard cock, a big hard cock, being slowly jacked back and forth. The guy at the urinal kept putting his finger to my glory hole, motioning me to stick mine through the opening. I finally got the message and did. He bent and sucked my cock to the hilt and got a super load out of me right away. I returned the favor and took several times longer to drain his load, a healthy one full of nut-flavored nutrition. I never saw his face, just his lovely pink fat cut cock.

The many times I returned to this john, I sometimes sat in the same booth, sometimes in the other. Never did I see toilet paper blocking the view (one of my pet peeves). Almost always I sucked cock. I never failed to drain the load of my objects there.

The various Trailways johns I have enjoyed over the years have proved to be steady suppliers of humps with healthy loads of cum. The most remarkable Trailways terminal I enjoyed was the new one (1960) in Waco, Texas, built in the aftermath of the late 1950s tornado. It was a wonder of pink marble and modern design. There were at least 10 booths all having very large glory holes put there by a sledge hammer. The space provided by the holes allowed any big-assed soul to place said ass through the hole and be fucked.

I was there only once, but for a long time—five hours in a layover between buses. A long time to suck and fuck. The large holes, at least a foot square, provided a panorama of sex in action. One could see all the way to the last booth. If a hard cock excited one, one could move to the next stall and suck or get fucked, or fuck the other player. I worked my way through all the booths in that five-hour layover.

The first one was next door—a cowboy type, long, brown, and rangy. He slung his long thin dick through the hole between us, his ass being played with by the kind soul in the next booth. He shot a big load of bittersweet cum to me.

The second soul I sucked at the Waco Trailways was a Chicano. Hard little body, scared, with hard fat little cock, not clipped, just the tip of the head showing when hard. Tip brownish pink with a big piss slit. Hot. He quickly stuffed it through the hole, allowing me to quickly drain his load.

The third soul was black. Big dick sticking through the hole, wanting more than my mouth could provide, so I wet my ass, turned, and allowed his big fat dick to sink all the way into my hot asshole.

Number four was a wonder, a short, cute, uncut Texas farm boy, long fat cock. In Waco for what? But got a wondrous blow job from a passer-through.

During the civil rights movement, I wandered into many Southern johns and occasionally sucked cock. One of the best was in a Greyhound john in Mississippi, which was active but segregated. Two johns stood side by side, one white, the other reading "colored." Between the two the wall was broken into a large hole, a very large hole. One could stick cock, balls, or ass completely through.

I sneaked into the colored john and waited, watching through the gigantic hole. A guy entered the other john, stood at the urinal jacking his big uncut meat. He stuck it through the hole, waiting, expecting a black mouth to suck it. He was surprised to receive a white mouth instead.

No blacks entered that john in Hattiesburg when I was there. Maybe they saw me in there and avoided coming in because of my race. But Oxford, home of Faulkner and Mississippi University, was different. There the johns in the Trailways station were unmarked except by gender (male/female). The male john was old, smelly, delightful (God I love that outhouse odor; the finest Parisian perfume can't compare). I waited there only moments before the first guy occupied the other stall. No glory hole or peeking. He started to play footsie. In a few minutes I motioned him under the partition. He slid all that great dark lower body, 10" of hard hot cock dripping slime, under the partition. After a few minutes of my tongue he shot his load.

In a few minutes another guy entered and slid his body beneath the partition and received identical attention. And another and another, until my mouth gave out. There are times when sucking cock after cock after cock never gets boring, but each blow job fades into the next. Only the unusual cock stays in my memory, or the tasty load.

Hope you enjoy the enclosed annual report of my company, with picture of yours truly. »«

SAILORS IN SAN DIEGO; NIGHT & DAY

I told you in another letter about some of San Diego's fabled public toilets back in the late 40s and early 50s. I spent so much time in those places, I'd like to think I could fill a book with anecdotes about them; but on reflection, I realize that of the hundreds of sexual encounters I had in them, most are beyond recall. Yet some linger in my mind.

For example, one day I was hanging out in a john just outside the main entrance to the famous zoo in San Diego's Balboa Park. I was sitting on one of the stools. I heard some people talking outside. It was a man with his wife and little daughter. They apparently were on their way to the zoo.

The guy came in the toilet, calling back to his family that he'd be out in just a jiffy. The urinals were along the wall opposite the toilets. None of the booths had a door.

He stood at the urinal directly in front of me and at a sideways angle sufficent to give me a glimpse of his dick. He looked at me hopefully with a hint of a smile. Surprised, I smiled back. It was all he needed. He strode right over and dropped his pants down around his thighs. He was extraordinarily handsome but his dick was extraordinarily small, like a little boy's. He wasn't in the least self conscious about it and drilled me in the mouth with it like a sewing machine.

His wife, still waiting outside, called after him to hurry up. He called out for her to hold her horses.

It didn't take him long. He shot a big, thick, hot load of cum out of that tiny dick, thanked me, shook my hand (!), and left, looking happy as a lark.

It thrilled me to do it while his wife and child were just a few feet away and I have never since scorned a small dick.

In the center of downtown San Diego is an old public square with a small fountain in the center called Horton Plaza. Across Broadway north of the square is the U.S. Grant Hotel, one of the best in the city. South of the square and facing it were two sleazy movie houses, now gone, and a bar called Bradley's which catered to sailors; sailors swarmed the area night and day.

One of the theatres and the hotel had cruisy men's rooms. I often sucked cock in the balcony of the movie house and would while away an hour or so in the john from time to time.

There was one Marine who was often in the john, young and good looking. I was never able to make it with him—not quite. He wanted no physical contact. There were small peek holes in the partitions between the toilets. He got off by having me, in the booth adjacent to his, bend over with my ass to the peek hole. He would jerk off looking at my asshole. He was often in there when I was and he always got off in the same way. Very frustrating for me; he wouldn't even return the favor by letting me beat off while looking at *his* asshole. But he was so handsome I was glad to help him out, even in so passive a way.

I'll never forget another odd incident that occurred in there. A sailor took the booth to the left of mine. The peek holes were very small, being the screw holes of a missing paper dispenser. Much of the time you could peek at your neighbor without his being aware of it. But this sailor became aware that I was peeking and put a piece of paper over the hole.

So I forgot about him and turned my attention to the fellow in the booth on the right of mine. About ten minutes later, something hot splashed against my left cheek. I turned just in time to see several long jets of cum spurt through the tiny hole, landing on my shirt and my bare legs. Too late, I put my mouth over the hole; the eruption was over. I had to content myself with licking up the few drops that were running down the partition just under the hole and scooping it up from where it had landed on my shirt and legs.

I wasn't sure just what his intentions had been. Had he changed his mind and been trying to get my attention? Or had he taken down the paper just in order to squirt cum all over me as an act of hostility? I was never sure, but I certainly regretted that so much of that heavy load had to go to waste.

Won't Give "Free Sample"

Considering how much time I spent in places like that, it is remarkable just how seldom I encountered any overt hostility in them. Once, I recall, a note that I passed under the partition was passed back with shit on it—he'd wiped his ass with it, and surely intended it as an insult. Actually, it thrilled me; and knowing that he was watching my reaction through the peek hole, I got back at him by tucking the paper into my mouth and swallowing it.

Another time, I was sucking cock at the urinal while four other guys were standing around watching. Suddenly someone came out of one of the booths and registered such a look of shock and disgust that everybody, including the guy I was sucking, fled the room.

I was embarrassed and a bit frightened as I stood up. I don't know why I didn't flee myself, but somehow I was getting mixed vibes from him. He was standing at the wash basin looking at me through narrowed eyes, unmistakably contemptuous. Yet I had the feeling he was torn between the impulse to beat me up and an impulse to let me suck *him,* or both.

161

But realizing that it was folly to wait to find out, I turned and left also. As I approached the door the butt of his cigarette whizzed by my ear, hit the door, and showered sparks. He had deftly shot the butt at me from between his fingers, barely missing me.

I was glad to get out unscathed but I've always wondered if, in fact, he would have let me suck him if I'd stayed.

If I were to choose the single most exciting encounter I've ever had in a public toilet, it would have to be the one described next. I had ensconced myself in one of the booths of the U.S. Grant Hotel across the Plaza from the movie houses. The men's room was off the main lobby and comparatively swank, with a long line of urinals and as many as eight booths, all in black marble.

A sailor was in the booth next to mine. I had passed some notes under the partition (there were no peek holes) and had received some affable replies. I wanted to take him home with me, but he wanted money. I was a student in those days and had no money. I kept trying to entice with promises of all the good things I'd do for him if he'd come. He was getting hornier and hornier and so was I.

Between notes, he was looking at a girlie magazine. Several times over, at my pleading, he stuck his dick under the partition, awkward but manageable, and at one point permitted me to stick my head under the partition. He moved his ass off the stool and lowered it onto my face so that I could lick him. Having just taken a shit, it wasn't too tidy, but it was by the time I'd finished licking it.

He was game for anything—piss, shit, I could blow him, anything, but for a price. He finally cut me off altogether (no more free samples, says he) and then departed.

I was heartsick with disappointment, but then I noticed he'd left behind the girlie magazine. I reached under and got it. I opened it to the centerfold and found that he had shot a simply stupendous load all over it. Long ropes of thick white cream all over it. I lapped it all up in a kind of delirium, not missing a drop, and shooting my own load.

Much as I would have liked to have made it with him for real, the encounter was intensely exciting just as it happened and over the years I've jerked off countless times thinking about it.

Vinny Likes Suck Holes Too.

Writing about my past experiences has made me realize how much my life (and everybody else's I suppose) has changed during the era of the AIDS plague. I had as promiscuous a youth as anyone ever had. I was always in the bars, on the streets, in the johns, movie balconies, and in the baths. Wherever sex was in flower, I was a bee after the nectar. So I was usually too busy finding new dicks and asses to have much time for old ones.

For me, that began to change back in the late 60s when I gave up drinking and stopped going to bars, then later gave up the baths when intestinal infections came to be so prevalent. So I became more dependent on men that I already knew. Now I am totally so.

Among these is Wes, whom I've known for more than 20 years and have made it with *weekly* during all that time. Familiarity, as far as I am concerned, definitely does not breed contempt, for Wes and my other "regulars" excite me more the longer I know them.

Wes is physically (and spiritually) as beautiful as any man I've ever known. The world's handsomest ass, a large, perfectly-formed dick, and the body of an athlete. One could scarcely get tired of him.

He was in his early 20s when I first met him, inexperienced but game for anything. My scat letch caught his fancy from the beginning and the lengths of tongue I've shoved up his ass would circle the globe—around the world for real.

Rusty I've known for 25 years and I see him with increasing frequency, now about every three weeks. Rusty, whose hair is a shade too red, whose skin is a shade too pale, and whose face is several shades too ethnic, is homely in the Woodly Allen tradition but sweet-natured, kind, and gentle.

He has a terrific body and cock. We are lock and key in our sexual proclivities, perfectly matched. An ardent top man in the scat scene who can be counted on to deliver *world class* product, every time.

He has been the author of some of the most elegantly formed, sculpted intestinal scrimshaw ever produced by man. The stuff of fantasy, but it took me many years to accommodate his homeliness. It was a major turnoff for a long time but now, I'm so turned on by him I look for him in other people (I've learned to *love* fiery red pubic hair) and often jerk off thinking of Woody Allen!

Vinny is a comparatively recent (1979) addition to my regulars. When I first met him he had a motorcycle and ran with a pack of Bensonhurst motorcycle punks, most of them younger than Vinny. Vinny is now in his 40s but his slim, muscular, almost hairless body could be that of a 19-year-old. Though half Irish and half Italian, his body is Japanese. His culture and character are 100% Italian.

He was comparatively new to gay life when I first met him. He had started letting guys blow him as a kind of "goof;" that is, as a way of humiliating the guy. But his experiences ultimately led to his acknowledging his own bisexuality.

He's cunt-crazy and always drives the latest model Cadillac as a lure. I never see him on Friday. That's his "pussy night"

"He's absolutely merciless . . . no matter how I choke."

It took him relatively little time to find out that the ultimate "goof" was shitting on people and he took to it with verve.

In the beginning, of course, he was doing a "goof" on me. That, in itself, was exciting to me. Over the years, we've grown to be good friends, and he is much less interested in doing the scat thing with me.

Actually, he wants to "marry" me. Like so many Italian men, he's macho to the hilt. Always bossing me around and making me wait on him. Sexually, he's absolutely merciless, concerned only with his own pleasure. Fucks me up the ass (which I hate, but he *insists*) with his small, *steel rod* of a dick. Pokes me just as brutally down the throat. He literally tries to strangle me when he comes. He jams his dick as far as he can get it down my throat, holds my head in place with a vise-like grip, and tries to squirt his load directly into my lungs (or so it would seem), no matter how I choke and gag.

He likes to ride on my back with me on all fours. I'm not into any kind of S/M role playing and the "Big Daddy" manner in so small a frame seemed ludicrous at first and it was hard not to see it as a kind of burlesque, even as I went along with it to please him. It was only when I realized that he wasn't playing a role, but was being genuinely himself, that I learned to respond to him appropriately.

When he's here I devote every moment to giving him pleasure and making him happy. He always tells me what he wants and I try to give it to him.

I lick his feet and armpits, tongue-fuck his asshole for hours on end, give him massages and oil rubs, suck his cock, and drink his piss.

From time to time, when he's especially horny, he'll feed me shit, and when he fucks me, even though I'm a much larger man than he is, he jerks me around in every imaginable position.

Perhaps I *should* "marry" him. While he is not notably bright, he has many elegant qualities of character and I admire and esteem him for a variety of reasons.

It doesn't hurt either that he recently came into a great deal of money. His mother died last year and left him a half million dollars and a couple of apartment houses.

He doesn't know how to manage it and needs me.

I've been surprised to find in myself something of the hausfrau he needs. But I couldn't do it full time and it's better to keep things as they are.

So that's it for my "regulars." Next time I'll write about my "irregulars." I have three of those also. »«

164

QUARTERMASTER CORPS

I have not written you for a long time as I'm wasting too much time (1) earning a living and (2) cruising for cock.

When I was in the U.S. Army, I had basic training in the Quartermaster Corps. There I met a couple of characters that remain interesting to me after years have passed.

One was a fellow called Preacher (because he was forever misquoting scripture). Preacher was very goodlooking and I could never understand his obsession with sin. Just about everything was a sin. Unfortunately, I was in the bunk next to Preacher's and I had to put up with his ranting.

Preacher had a long uncut cock with a lot of foreskin and believe me it smelled. He took regular showers and I had seen him soaping his cock, but I don't think he had washed under that long foreskin in his life. I would sit on my bunk writing a letter home and perhaps Preacher would be sitting nearby on his bunk cleaning his rifle and the strong smell of cock cheese would waft over. Preacher had the end bunk and there was nobody on the other side of him to complain. I was the one who got the full impact of Preacher's cockhead cheese.

We were all tired after a day's marching or whatever, and I usually went to bed at lights out. I would lay on my side and jack off, using a pair of socks as a cum rag. If you got semen on your sheets, somebody would notice and make fun of you. Usually the socks were not completely dry by morning, but my Army boots hurt my feet so badly I always wore 2 pairs of socks anyway so I would put a dry pair on first and then the spermy pair on over them and that worked okay. Washing the cum-rag socks was a problem though.

Preacher really had a problem with that big uncut cock of his. When he went to bed, he would tuck in the sheet on both sides and put his arms outside the sheet. Several times Preacher had told me that "self abuse" was sinful so I figured he was trying to not touch himself. Sometimes if I glanced toward his bunk, I could see the sheet tenting up, and sometimes I would hear him sigh or moan softly as if in frustration that he couldn't control his cock and balls. Eventually his right hand would go under the sheet, the sheet would move up and down for 5 or 10 minutes, then Preacher would get out of his bunk and rush towards the latrine. When he returned he usually dropped to his knees by his bunk and I guess asked for forgiveness.

During the first few weeks of basic training, we were restricted to the Army camp, and for some periods restricted to the company area. On the 3rd week, I was issued a weekend pass and went into town for the first time. I had gotten married about a month before my induction but I had no idea of looking for pussy. The main thing was just to

165

get away from the Army for a weekend, but I knew I wouldn't let an available cock or warm male mouth get by me.

The bus was overcrowded and I had to stand all the way. About half way to town I realized that the soldier standing behind me seemed to be massaging my butt with his groin. I didn't mind as long as it wasn't too obvious. When we got to town, he suggested we hang out together as neither of us knew the town. That was okay with me. He insisted we get a room at the YMCA so we would have somewhere to sleep if we got tired or loaded or whatever.

The clerk wanted to put us in a dormitory but Cowboy,'my friend, persuaded him to give us a room by telling him other guys would laugh at our meditations and prayers. Cowboy was a lanky, bowlegged lad (we were all about 18 years old), from out west somewhere. He was very sexy and I had jacked off in my bunk thinking about him— licking his big cock, which I had seen in the shower, or putting my cock between the firm cheeks of his butt.

When we got to the room, Cowboy said he wanted to rest for awhile. He lay down on his bunk and pulled his pants and underpants off. "I just have to give this thing some air," he said.

I wasn't at all sure of Cowboy, or at least I hadn't been, but I started to undress and the minute he saw my dick he was off the bunk and we were in each other's arms, kissing and trying to get our tongues down each other's throats. Instant true love.

"Most of us wore only underpants or nothing at all."

I had had some sex with boys and men on the farm, but not all that much, and I remember that weekend with Cowboy (and 3 weekends that followed) as a glorious honeymoon. Cowboy and I were perfect sex buddies. We did everything to each other, and for each other. It was the first time that I sucked and got sucked, fucked and got fucked. It was beautiful.

Also, we were both very affectionate and just about wore the skin off our faces with kissing and hugging and rubbing and cuddling (Oh, heaven!)

We spent most of that first weekend in that little room, going to the showers a few times to wash off the sweat and semen and shit. We went out only for food and smuggled back candy bars and snacks in our pockets for energy.

Back in the barracks, sometimes our platoon had nothing to do but just sit on our bunks and tell or listen to dirty jokes. Pussy jokes. Queer jokes, some very offensive, some very funny—and some very sexy.

With all the inactivity and the dirty talk, everybody was plenty horny. Most of us wore only underpants or nothing at all. I remember one beautiful pink little guy who threw a hard on during some dirty joke telling. He just sat there, listening to the dirty talk with his cock pointing to the sky, completely naked. Aloysius, the Hulk of our platoon, told him to get some pants on before he got tooth marks all over him.

Even when we were restricted to the area, some fellows sneaked away and discovered the tavern. One night a lot of us sneaked to the tavern, drank more than in the rest of our lives, and got very sick. I was okay until I went to bed, at which point the bed started spinning and I threw up. I was not the only one. The next morning the guys who were not sick cleaned up the mess and forced us hangover guys to take cold showers. Somebody went to the PX store and bought air sprays and had the place smelling like Lysol and roses by the time the first non-com came to have us police the area. But a few lads were still gagging and throwing up, so he insisted that some of us report on sick call. He suspected either an epidemic or tainted food. The non-com delegated one of our group to march us to sick call. When we got there we saw dozens of sick guys waiting so we turned around and went back to our barracks and went to bed.

The hero of this little episode was a lad from a large Eastern city (guess which) who had been a member of a boy gang which had military-type discipline and who had persuaded some of the guys to clean up our mess and try to get us in condition so that our little drinking bout did not come to the attention of those in authority.

Later, he developed this idea further. If something happened to one of the men in our platoon, we tried to handle it among ourselves. Incidents such as jealousy, fighting, suspected stealing, and, yes, sex, were discussed quietly among us and never even came to the attention of the cadre corporals who had rooms in our barracks. Some fellows just naturally take to leadership in the Army.

Right in the middle of basic training, the N.Y. lad was reassigned to the Adjutant General's Office (I think) and the interior discipline of our platoon fell apart.

I was broken hearted when orders were posted and Cowboy and I were on different orders and although neither of us knew where we were going, we knew we would no longer be together. »«

"IT TASTED SWEATY AND A LITTLE PISSY."

I met Ray in early 1969. He was 22 and had just returned from Vietnam, where he'd served as a lieutenant in the Army. I was an 18-year-old who knew I was homosexual but had never sucked a dick.

We were both freshmen at a small liberal arts college in Pennsylvania. Ray and I lived in the same dormitory; his room was two doors down from mine.

The first time I saw him was in the bathroom. I walked in to piss and there he was, standing at a sink, stripped to the waist, shaving.

Now, even though I'd had no sexual experiences with guys, I knew full well why I liked dorm life—you always got to see naked male flesh. In my one semester of college I'd already spied some fantastic meat in the showers, rooms, and even the hallways—some of the more exhibitionistic studs liked to walk around bareass, showing off their dicks and fat nuts, not to mention their fine young physiques.

None of these hunks turned my head like Ray did. They were mostly my age—maybe the oldest guy on our floor was 20—but Ray was 22, a real mature number, in my view—and he was built: six feet tall, broad shouldered, thickly muscled, and hairy. His rugged appeal was heightened by several small scars on his shoulders and back—from shrapnel, I later learned. I nodded "hello" to him (I think I was too intimidated to start a conversation) and he hello-ed me back.

My roommate told me that "the big guy is Stick's new roommate" (Stick was what we called this skinny nerd who lived a couple of rooms away).

"Have you met him yet?" asked Ken, my roommate. "He's a wild guy. From the South I think."

Ken was right on both counts. Although Ray's family had lived in Pennsylvania for about 10 years, they were originally from Alabama. And Ray turned out to be a wild one, a rowdy old boy of Scottish, Irish, and Indian background.

The two of us didn't have much in common. I was Italian, from a Northeastern city, and at that time a hippy with shaggy hair and my first beard; Ray's background was rural and Southern and he'd been an Army officer, in Nam no less. I hated the war and had no intention of going into the Army if I were drafted.

But whatever our differences, we hit if off real well. It turned out he hated the war too—he'd seen too many of his buddies end up in body bags and too many Vietnamese peasants char-broiled with napalm—and he loathed the Army brass.

I was about the only one of us callow youths who wanted to hear what Nam was like (everybody else either didn't give a shit or else didn't want to hear about a situation they had escaped via their student deferments), so we spent many nights up late, taking amphetamines, drinking beer, and rapping.

Ray didn't talk only about how shitty the war was. He liked to regale me with stories of his sexual exploits with nurses, other women Army personel, and Vietnamese hookers.

"I pretended to like his wife."

My favorite story was the one about the night he and his best buddy fucked their brains out in a whorehouse; they switched whores, at one point, mixing their cum in the women's twats. That little narrative gave me plenty of jack-off fodder.

My voyeurism gave me more inspiration. The toilet stalls in the dorm bathrooms faced the showers, so anybody sitting on the bowl could peep through the cracks of the door and check out the showering studs. I spent an inordinate amount of time on the toilet peeping at naked men. Sometimes I think my grades would have been higher had the layout of the dorm bathrooms been different.

Naturally I made sure I got my ass in my favorite stall when I knew Ray was going to shower. The first time I saw him bareass my heart was racing and my body literally shook. I'd already seen his powerful and furry torso but the whole package just did me in. His cock was on the short side but very fat; it jutted out at a nice angle, resting on a pair of big fat balls. His legs were huge, hairy tree-trunks, the most muscular I'd ever seen. The ass was small, compact, and not too hairy.

After he dried himself and left (I was terrified that he would know it was me sitting on the stall), I jacked my dick to a fast but satisfying orgasm.

Ray and I stayed friends throughout college, though we were never as close as we were that first year. He moved off-campus when we were sophomores and I didn't see him that often anymore. When we were seniors he got married. I pretended to like his wife and we got along pretty well, but I really disliked her. She seemed an insipid little nag to me, always complaining about Ray's drinking and dope-smoking, always wanting to tame him and make him into a good, boring husband. I guess I was just jealous that she was getting his dick, not me.

The three years after college were wasted ones for me. I moved to Boston, had an on-again off-again love affair with a hunky but very fucked-up Irish Catholic guy, and when the tortured relationship ended moved to Connecticut, where my parents lived.

I found out that Ray and his wife had moved to a nearby town and were living in a rented house with Stick and his wife. So I paid them all a visit. I still had the fucked-up Irishman on my mind and my visit to Ray had no hidden (sexual) agenda. But when I saw him a lot of the old feelings came back. He looked great, with his moderately long hair and full reddish-brown beard. It was a hot July night and he was wearing only a pair of blue jean cutoffs. It was 1969 all over again. My dick started to harden in my pants.

Over the next few years we became real tight again, even more so than we'd been in college. After Stick and his wife got divorced, I helped Ray and his old lady move into their new house.

At first his wife and I got along okay but as I began to spend more time hanging out with Ray, things got tense between me and her. She clearly resented the situation and she'd sometimes let the two of us know it, sometimes in indirect ways, such as irritated little outbursts that ostensibly had nothing to do with the fact that she felt neglected. But the underlying message was pretty clear.

I guess she had a reason to dislike the situation and I suppose I had some malicious intent. But she was such a tiresome little twat; I never really felt guilty when she'd be home alone Saturday evenings watching TV and stuffing her fat face with junk food while Ray and I were out riding around, visiting our buddies, and carousing.

All this buddy-buddy shit took a new turn one drunken night. A new turn, but not an unexpected one. Ray's wife was away visiting her mother. We were drinking beer, smoking pot, and blasting the stereo. Too drunk to drive home, I was to sleep over on the sofabed in Ray's living room.

Sometime after midnight Ray passed out on the opened sofabed and I, too drunk to give a fuck about what he might think, jumped in with him. He was lying on his back, his shirt half unbottoned, exposing his big hairy chest. I reached over and started stroking him. He didn't stir. Then I put my hand on his crotch and squeezed. He still didn't wake up so I kept squeezing and rubbing it until I felt his dick getting hard.

At this point he stirred and mumbled, "What are you doing, man?"

"What do you think? Grabbing your cock."

"Why you doing that?" he drawled slowly.

"Because you like it."

He didn't say a word as I opened his pants and pulled them down. He wasn't wearing underwear, so I just dived down and popped his meat in my mouth—seven years after I'd first wanted to. It tasted funky-delicious, sweaty, and a little pissy.

After a few minutes of fervent sucking I asked, "How does that feel?"

Ever the wiseass, he replied, "Like you're sucking me off."

"Do you like it, asshole?"

"Oh, yeah, man. Keep it up."

I continued slurping on his rod, which was iron-hard and drooling like a baby. (These were two of the things I came to like most about making it with Ray: the implacable hardness of hard ons and his pre-seminal flow. He was almost always leaking before I even touched his dick. When he did wear Jockey shorts, there would be a round wet spot in the fly from dick juice.)

As I worked him over with my mouth, I groped his balls and big legs. He started to hump his hips and grind his ass.

"Take off my pants," he said, "so I can move my legs." After I got his jeans off and tossed them on the floor, he spread his legs wide, making it easier for me to suck his balls and sniff his ass. While I serviced him, I got my dick out of my pants and started whacking it. This went on for a half-hour or so. We were both having a good time, but it didn't seem like my sucking was going to make Ray bust his nuts. He gently pushed me off his dick and started pumping it with his big hairy hand. I continued to lick his nuts while I jerked off.

When the first blast of cum shot out of his piss-hole I dived on his dick and made sure he shot his load into my mouth. I swallowed it all, loving it. This startled him a bit; I don't think he expected me to eat his cum.

You might think that after this fairly spectacular start we would become steady suck-partners right away. But it didn't work out like that.

For weeks we pretended that it hadn't happened. Neither of us spoke about it or gave each other any hint that we wanted to do it again.

Then one Saturday night, when we were hanging out at his house, drinking and playing his stereo, I got my nerve up.

"Look," I said, grabbing his arm. "Are we ever going to get in on again, or what?"

He was taken aback by my directness, but he had a ready answer: "Yeah, sure, man. Why not?"

I immediately grabbed his crotch and started squeezing. It hardened almost instantaneously. There we were, both of us drunk and high on pot, me jerking him off through his pants with his wife watching TV in another room.

"His mouth hung open, his chest was heaving."

I got scared—the last thing I wanted was to have her walk in on us—and stopped beating Ray's meat. He was none too happy about the interruption.

"You got me all excited, and now you're going to stop?"

I explained to him that his wife's presence nearby inhibited me. I would make it up to him, I promised, by sucking him off on Wednesday, when his wife would be working late.

That Wednesday session was probably the hottest time we ever had together. probably because it was planned and not a spontanous happening in a drunken moment.

When I arrived at Ray's house in the late afternoon, I was literally shaking with excitement. Four days of anticipation will do that to you.

I could tell that Ray was all keyed up too, by the way he paced around and smoked cigarette after cigarette.

Yet it almost didn't happen. We stood around in the kitchen, sipping beers, both of us feeling a bit awkward.

"What do you want to do?" Ray asked in a hushed voice.

"Let's go in the living room."

We sat on the sofa, close but slightly apart, like two nervous teenagers on a first date. I admitted my nervousness.

"Yeah, I know," Ray said. "I'm a lot looser myself when I'm drunk."

But horniness won out. I reached over and grabbed Ray's crotch. To my delight, he had a big hard on.

"Christ," I said, "you're hard as hell." He laughed. The unmistakeable evidence in his pants told me that he wanted this as much as I did, maybe even more.

I unbuckled his belt, pushing aside his pants. I *had* to strip him. I reached into his jockeys and my fingers got wet when they grazed his dick head. Ray raised his hips so I could yank down his pants and shorts. I pulled them down to his ankles and knelt on the rug in front of him. Then I pushed his T shirt above his nipples so I could play with them while I sucked his cock. God, I loved doing him. I revelled in every lick of his dick, in the musky smell rising from his balls and asshole, in his appreciative moans and ass-wriggling. At one point I took his dick out of my mouth and jacked it, staring into his glazed eyes.

"It's going to do it, man," he said breathlessly. I popped the wet rod back into my mouth to get the load. He came hard (another of his endearing attributes); I could feel the shots ricocheting against the

172

back of my throat. As he shot I looked up at him. His head was thrown back, his mouth hung open, and his chest, streaked with sweat, was heaving.

I was amazed at how long his dick stayed hard after he came. A bonus for me. I just kept on sucking until he asked me to stop.

"That was far out," he said, sounding awed.

A week later we had another rousing workout. (Wednesday became our regular sex day because his wife always worked late on Wednesdays. We also got together every other Saturday. This went on for three years.) When I walked into Ray's house, he was on the phone, chatting with his wife. While he was talking I unbuttoned his shirt and played with his chest hair and nipples. He cut short the conjugal chat.

"What do you want to do?" he said, his voice husky with anticipation.

"Let's use the sofabed," I said.

He threw the cushions off the sofa in a hurry and pulled out the mattress. He then went upstairs to piss. When he returned he stood close to me, putting a hand on my shoulder. He looked into my eyes, then gazed down at his crotch. His pants were open and his hard on stood up straight in his jockeys. There was a wet spot on the shorts, right where dick head met cotton. I moved to pull down his pants but he stopped me. He took them off, along with his socks. Then he got into bed, wearing only his unbuttoned shirt.

"Some of it leaked out of my mouth."

"The shirt too," I ordered.

"The shirt?" He sounded surprised. There he was just about totally bareassed, with a big dripping hard on, and he suddenly gets modest—as if to surrender the shirt would be depraved. I had to laugh. He realized the ridiculousness of the situation, laughed too, and stripped off his shirt.

He lay back in bed, his hands under his head. His balls looked full and taut. I tore off my clothes and jumped in with him. We humped, groped, and fondled each other. We were real hungry. Then he had an inspiration. He reached over to the table by the sofa and snatched up a small silver packet and the rolled-up dollar lying next to it. Inside the tinfoil packet was a half gram of good cocaine. We snorted it up and smoked half a joint.

While we ingested the dope, I worked his dick with my free hand. When we got back to sex, we were ready to tear each other apart. I licked him all over. I sucked his nipples and occasionally bit them, making him cry out. I fingered his sweaty asshole, making him jump. And of course I sucked his juicy piece and licked his balls.

All he did to me was grope me and jerk my dick but that was okay; I was so overjoyed to be doing all these wild things, this guy that I'd lusted after for years, that I cared little about reciprocation. His pleasure was mine and boy was he enjoying himself. When he shot his load it was so copious that some of it leaked out of the corners of my mouth.

Afterwards I said there's nothing quite like a cocaine orgasm.

"Shit," he said, "I thought I was going to have a heart attack."

On another occasion I even sucked him off while his wife was home. We'd been drinking beer, as usual, and Ray went to piss off the back porch steps. When he hadn't returned after about five minutes, I went out to see what was the problem. He was standing there at the top of the stairs in a pissing stance, his legs spread and his hand at his crotch. But no piss flowed.

"What's the matter? Too hard to piss?"

"Yeah.'

Good old Ray, hard as usual.

I stroked his meat for a few minutes, then got down in front of him and started sucking.

"Shit, man, what if somebody sees us?"

I didn't give a fuck about the neighbors (whose house was several hundred yards away anyway) and just kept on eating his meat.

Suddenly his knees started to buckle and I tasted a salty fluid on my tongue.

"Look out, man," he exclaimed several times, warning me that an explosion was imminent. He wanted me to take his dick out of my mouth but I paid no attention. Within seconds he shot an ample load into my hungry mouth.

After he came I asked why he wanted me to stop.

"Because I didn't know if you were going to get cum or piss," he said, a bit abashed. I just laughed. I was so charged up that I probably would've taken both, though I didn't tell him that.

BOOKS FROM LEYLAND PUBLICATIONS / G.S PRESS

- ☐ **MEN LOVING MEN: A Gay Sex Guide & Consciousness Book** by Mitch Walker. New revised edition. 40 + photos. Perfect gift. $16.95.
- ☐ **MEATMEN Anthology of Gay Male Comics.** Tom of Finland, Donelan, etc. Large sized books / $17.95 each. Circle books wanted. Volumes 1, 3, 4, 5, 6, 7, 8, 9, 10, 11, 12, 13, 14, 15, 16, 17.
- ☐ **ENLISTED MEAT / WARRIORS & LOVERS / MILITARY SEX / MARINE BIOLOGY: True Homosexual Military Stories.** Vols. 1, 2, 3, 4. $15.95 each. Circle books wanted. Soldiers / sailors / marines tell all about their sex lives.
- ☐ **SEX BEHIND BARS / BOYS BEHIND BARS / THE BOYS OF VASELINE ALLEY** (3 Vols.) by Robert N. Boyd. True stories of male-male prison sex, and street hustling. $16.95 each. Circle books wanted.
- ☐ **MANPLAY / YOUNG NUMBERS / HUMONGOUS / 10½ INCHES / BOYS BOYS BOYS! / STUDFLESH / BOYS WILL BE BOYS / EIGHTEEN & OVER: True Gay Encounters.** Vols. 3–10. Circle books wanted. Hot male-male sex stories. $12.95 each.
- ☐ **LUST** True Gay Encounters. Vol. 1 $16.95.
- ☐ **LEATHERMEN SPEAK OUT** Vols. 1 & 2. Ed. Jack Ricardo. 50 leather dads & sons, slaves & masters reveal their S&M sex encounters. $16.95 ea.
- ☐ **SIR! MORE SIR! The Joy of S&M** by Master Jackson. Complete guide to S&M / leather sex with sections on bondage, spanking, whipping, tit torture, water sports, roles etc. $16.95.
- ☐ **TRASH / TRUCKER / SEXSTOP / HEADSTOPS / HOT TRICKS / MEAT RACK: True Revelations from 18 Wheeler** Vols. 1 to 6. Ed. by John Dagion. True sex stories. Circle books wanted. $12.95 each.
- ☐ **ROCK ON THE WILD SIDE: Gay Male Images in Popular Music of the Rock Era** by Wayne Studer. Illustrated. $17.95.
- ☐ **GAY ROOTS: Anthology of Gay History, Sex, Politics & Culture.** Vols. 1 & 2. Edited by Winston Leyland. More than 100 + writers. Vol. 1 won Lambda Book Award 1992 for best gay book of the year. Illustrated. More than 1000 pages total. Vol. 1: $25.95; Vol. 2 $22.95 (or special price of $39.95 for both, save $9.00).
- ☐ **HIGH CAMP: A Guide to Gay Cult & Camp Films** by Paul Roen. Illustrated reviews of gay camp films over the past 50 years—such stars as Bette Davis, Joan Crawford, James Dean, Steve Reeves, Judy Garland. $17.95.
- ☐ **CALAMUS LOVERS / DRUM BEATS** Two books on the gay life of Walt Whitman: his love for soldiers in Civil War etc. Illustrated. $11.95 each.
- ☐ **MEAT / CUM / JUICE / WADS** Best selling **True Homosexual Experiences from S.T.H.** edited by Boyd McDonald $13.95 each (4 vols.). Circle books wanted.
- ☐ **MILKIN' THE BULLS and other Hot Hazing Stories** by John Barton. Stories of military school, sexual hazing, etc. $16.95.
- ☐ **ORGASMS / HOT STUDS / SINGLEHANDED:** Homosexual Encounters from First Hand. $12.95 each (3 vols.). Circle books wanted.
- ☐ **THE KISS OF THE WHIP: Explorations in SM** by Jim Prezwalski $17.95.
- ☐ **GHOST KISSES Gothic Gay Romance Stories** by Gregory L. Norris $14.95.

TO ORDER: Check book(s) wanted (or list them on a separate sheet) and send check / money order to Leyland Publications, PO Box 410690, San Francisco, CA 94141. **Postage included in prices quoted.** Calif. residents add 8¼ % sales tax. Mailed in unmarked book envelopes. Add $1 for complete catalogue.

AIDS RISK REDUCTION GUIDELINES
FOR HEALTHIER SEX

As given by Bay Area Physicians for Human Rights

NO RISK: *Most of these activities involve only skin-to-skin contact, thereby avoiding exposure to blood, semen, and vaginal secretions. This assumes there are no breaks in the skin.* 1) Social kissing (dry). 2) Body massage, hugging. 3) Body to body rubbing (frottage). 4) Light S&M (without bruising or bleeding). 5) Using one's own sex toys. 6) Mutual masturbation (male or external female). Care should be taken to avoid exposing the partners to ejaculate or vaginal secretions. Seminal, vaginal and salivary fluids should not be used as lubricants.

LOW RISK: *In these activities small amounts of certain body fluids might be exchanged, or the protective barrier might break causing some risk.* 1) Anal or vaginal intercourse with condom. Studies have shown that HIV does not penetrate the condom in simulated intercourse. Risk is incurred if the condom breaks or if semen spills into the rectum or vagina. The risk is further reduced if one withdraws before climax. 2) Fellatio interruptus (sucking, stopping before climax). Pre-ejaculate fluid may contain HIV. Saliva or other natural protective barriers in the mouth may inactivate virus in pre-ejaculate fluid. Saliva may contain HIV in low concentration. The insertive partner should warn the receptive partner before climax to prevent exposure to a large volume of semen. If mouth or genital sores are present, risk is increased. Likewise, action which causes mouth or genital injury will increase risk. 3) Fellatio with condom (sucking with condom) Since HIV cannot penetrate an intact condom, risk in this practice is very low unless breakage occurs. 4) Mouth-to-mouth kissing (French kissing, wet kissing) Studies have shown that HIV is present in saliva in such low concentration that salivary exchange is unlikely to transmit the virus. Risk is increased if sores in the mouth or bleeding gums are present. 5) Oral-vaginal or oral-anal contact with protective barrier. e.g. a latex dam, obtainable through a local dental supply house, may be used. Do not reuse latex barrier, because sides of the barrier may be reversed inadvertently. 6) Manual anal contact with glove (manual anal (fisting) or manual vaginal (internal) contact with glove). If the glove does not break, virus transmission should not occur. However, significant trauma can still be inflicted on the rectal tissues leading to other medical problems, such as hemorrhage or bowel perforation. 7) Manual vaginal contact with glove (internal). See above.

MODERATE RISK: *These activities involve tissue trauma and/or exchange of body fluids which may transmit HIV or other sexually transmitted disease.* 1) Fellatio (sucking to climax). Semen may contain high concentrations of HIV and if absorbed through open sores in the mouth or digestive tract could pose risk. 2) Oral-anal contact (rimming). HIV may be contained in blood-contaminated feces or in the anal rectal lining. This practice also poses high risk of transmission of parasites and other gastrointestinal infections. 3) Cunnilingus (oral-vaginal contact). Vaginal secretions and menstrual blood have been shown to harbor HIV, thereby causing risk to the oral partner if open lesions are present in the mouth or digestive tract. 4) Manual rectal contact (fisting). Studies have indicated a direct association between fisting and HIV infection for both partners. This association may be due to concurrent use of recreational drugs, bleeding, pre-fisting semen exposure, or anal intercourse with ejaculation. 5) Sharing sex toys. 6) Ingestion of urine. HIV has not been shown to be transmitted via urine; however, other immunosuppressive agents or infections may be transmitted in this manner.

HIGH RISK: *These activities have been shown to transmit HIV.* 1) Receptive anal intercourse without condom. All studies imply that this activity carries the highest risk of transmitting HIV. The rectal lining is thinner than that of the vagina or the mouth thereby permitting ready absorption of the virus from semen or pre-ejaculate fluid to the blood stream. One laboratory study suggests that the virus may enter by direct contact with rectal lining cells without any bleeding. 2) Insertive anal intercourse without condom. Studies suggest that men who participate only in this activity are at less risk of being infected than their partners who are rectally receptive; however the risk is still significant. It carries high risk of infection by other sexually transmitted diseases. 3) Vaginal intercourse without condom.